CREATIVE
DESIGN
· in ·
CROCHET

CREATIVE DESIGN · in · CROCHET

PAULINE TURNER

B. T. BATSFORD LTD · London

ISBN 0 7134 1197X (limp)

Typeset by Tek-Art Ltd, London SE20
and printed in Great Britain by
The Anchor Press Ltd
Tiptree, Essex
for the publishers
B.T. Batsford Ltd,
4 Fitzhardinge Street
London W1H 0AH

Contents

Acknowledgements

My grateful and totally inadequate thanks go to: Sue, Meryl, Tracey and Harry for modelling the garments so beautifully; Pamela for testing patterns and burning the midnight oil, plus Mary, Hilary and Louise; Paul Callis, the photographer, who did such an excellent job, often under severe difficulties; Dorothy who had to make sense of an illegible script and also kept me up to date with the timetable, allowing me *no* excuses for delay; Marian, the layman who taught herself to crochet whilst the book was in script form and was thus responsible for refining it; Mabel for permitting me to use her story concerning crochet; Kathleen and Mr Stell who gave me the initial confidence to accept the challenge; Rita of the Ashdell Restaurant, Cleveleys; my colleagues who proof-read; the many others who bolstered that confidence when it began to flag, and to all my students everywhere, without whom this book could not have been written.

Abbreviations and Terms

UK

st	stitch
cl	cluster
lp	loop
patt	pattern
yoh	yarn over hook
inc	increase
dec	decrease
tog	together
bet	between
gr	group
sp	space
rnd	round
rs	right side
ws	wrong side
rh	right hand
lh	left hand
MS	main shade
1st C	first contrast
2nd C	second contrast
DK	double knit

Chart for crochet terms

UK		**USA**	
ch	chain		
ss	slip stitch	sl st	
dc	double crochet	sc	single crochet
cr st	crab stitch		
tr	treble	dc	double crochet
Rtr	raised treble	Rdc	raised double crochet
RtrF	forward raised treble	RdcF	forward raised double crochet
RtrB	backward raised treble	RtrB	backward raised treble
3trcl	three treble cluster	3dccl	three double crochet cluster
4trcl	four treble cluster	4dccl	four double crochet cluster
dtr	double treble	tr	treble
tr tr	triple treble	dtr	double treble
quad tr	quadruple treble	tr tr	triple treble
htr	half treble	hdc	half double crochet

Foreword

Crochet has existed as a homecraft for many years, but as a creative art it is relatively new. It is only within the last ten years or so that people have begun to explore the potential of crochet techniques and designers to make use of the various combinations of stitches, yarns and hooks to create new and exciting effects. The aim of this book is to tackle some of the recurring problems and untangle some of the mysteries concerning crochet that my students have raised over the years and to show that crochet is one of the simplest crafts there is. Since I could not hope to cover all the questions that have been answered during this period, I have chosen to comply with the oft requested plea to produce something that will enable people to teach themselves crochet, and at the same time, explore and discover crochet's versatility for themselves.

Each chapter covers a different basic process – be it a stitch or technique – so that by the end of the chapter you are familiar with its operation and know how it will react as a fabric. You should also have been made aware of the many possible uses to which it can be put. Each chapter will be divided into four sections: Section A shows how to work the stitch or process, Section B gives experiments for you to try, to enable you to discover for yourself how the work changes with different yarns, hook sizes and hook insertions, Section C contains patterns that concentrate on newly learned techniques, and Section D gives suggestions for you to explore and how to commence designing for yourself.

Sections A and C are written in a way familiar to most people, with photographs and line drawings showing the process in Section A, and patterns written in a style similar to those purchased in yarn shops in Section C. Section B is particularly suitable for those with inquiring minds who do not want to learn to crochet by copying, but by understanding how stitches are likely to react in different situations. Section D opens the doors for you to put what you have learnt into practice and gives you guidelines as to how to exploit your own creative capabilities to produce garments that are your own individual creation.

USA readers will find any variation in terminology placed in brackets alongside the UK term.

There are no rules in this book, only guidelines and suggestions to help you discover for yourself the pleasure and satisfaction that crochet can bring at whatever level of competence you achieve. It is up to you to establish your own rules and once you have mastered the basic techniques the door is open to you to exploit the versatility that the craft of crochet offers.

I First Principles

There are no rigid rules in crochet, only good ways and bad ways; the good ways work, the bad ways cause all manner of complications. This chapter concerns refining basic techniques and elaborating that crochet know-how which sometimes causes confusion. The following recommendations have been found to work with a few hundred people, but if in the past you have tried to crochet and are comfortable when holding a hook and yarn in your own particular way, and if the resulting tension (gauge) is correct, then please continue to use your way and ignore those instruction given here.

THE HOOK

Since holding and controlling a pencil comes naturally to the majority of us, it will be easier to control a crochet hook if one holds it like a pencil. Of the many crochet hooks available, it is the conventional hook which is the best to learn with (*diagram 1*).

If you look closely at this crochet hook you can see that it narrows towards the hook head. It also has a section with a uniform diameter which is normally referred to as the 'stem'. It is the stem part that is responsible for the tension (gauge) of the crochet being worked. Any loops or yarn placed round the crochet hook should fit the circumference of the stem exactly. If the loops are too large, the work will be bigger than expected. Conversely, if you work on the narrow part near the hook head, then your work will be smaller.

Some hooks on the market have a means of extending the handle of the hook. There appears to be no advantage in this as it only adds weight, not mobility, to the hook. The critical part of the hook is the stem. Should you suffer from rheumatism or arthritis, a hook with a metal stem and a plastic handle has been found to be the most comfortable to use, as the plastic is warm to the touch and the metal is smooth to use.

When one starts to crochet, gifts are often made of hooks that have lain unused in a drawer at home for many years. These will be made of metal, wood or bone. Bone and wood hooks are lightweight, smooth and warm to use, but as they do not have a straight length of stem on which to form the loops, it may be better to use a modern hook in the initial stages of learning whilst gaining confidence in producing uniform loop sizes.

If you wish to find out the size of a crochet hook, simply insert the hook into a knitting needle gauge and where the stem of the hook fits snugly into a hole, the measure given is the size for that hook.

You will find a conversion chart for crochet hooks in Appendix I which may help if you are using old or foreign patterns, yet possess only modern crochet hooks. Alternatively, you may own some different styles of hook(s) which you would like to use with other

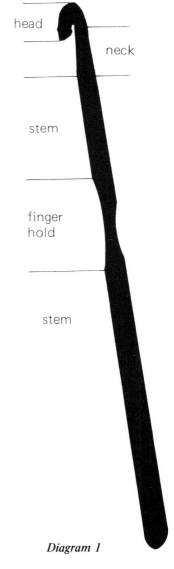

head

neck

stem

finger hold

stem

Diagram 1

patterns. It is possible that by the time you have followed the suggested route in this book, you may never need to use a crochet pattern, and the hook you do use will be purely a matter of personal choice.

YARN

The following are some guidelines that can be considered when taking the first tentative steps with a new process, but please do remember to try anything at all that takes your fancy when you are familiar with the basic technique, including such items as ribbon, rope, strips of leather and fabric, string, offcuts from a mill, or wire, as well as the usual cotton, wool, linen, silk, man-made yarns and the multitudinous mixtures of fibres available in hanks, balls, or cones.

a Aran yarn, whether pure wool or a mixture of wool and man-made fibre, has a crispness that enables it, once it has been worked up, to hold its shape and to show the stitch definition to advantage. This is perhaps the best of all yarns to use when making the very first attempt at a new process or structural idea.

b Silky yarns tend to slip and have difficulty holding their form.

c Hairy yarns can hide the stitch construction, but what is possibly worse, if you have to pull back any part of the work, the actual process of pulling back can be long and tedious and can also result in yarn loss.

d If your eyesight is not good, or if you suffer from stiff joints in the hands, fine yarns can be difficult to handle.

e Similarly, black and very dark colours can cause problems with the eyes, particularly if working in artificial light. Shiny metal hooks can be an advantage with the darker yarns.

f Pure nylon yarn has a tendency to stretch, and until you feel confident in holding the yarn so that it flows evenly and without too much drag through the fingers, it may be advisable to avoid this type of yarn.

g The final group of yarns to select with caution when making tentative steps into the unknown, are the slubbed, bouclé, chenille and other very textured yarns — not because these do not produce interesting results, but because a beginner cannot be sure whether it is the yarn that has done the work or the crocheter.

One of the delightful things about crochet is the ease with which it copes with unusual yarns. For example, chenille has a habit of catching against itself in knitting, but this is not so when crocheting. Another yarn that is great fun to crochet with is the fine yarn with huge slubs incorporated at infrequent intervals.

By following the suggested route and taking particular note of the B and D sections in each chapter, you should be able to see for yourself how yarns react with each other, with different hooks and with different stitches. So, by the end of the book you should have gained sufficient insight to have found your own area of crochet and be eager and equipped to explore that part of it more fully for yourself. You will probably have also realized, however, that to limit yourself to any one particular area too exclusively is to reject the wealth of opportunities that crochet offers, and I hope you will be inspired to go on trying out and discovering new combinations.

HOLDING THE WORK

The important thing is to find a way of holding the yarn which allows it to flow steadily with an even tautness through the fingers and does not cause the arm or fingers to ache.

With the palm face down, bring the yarn from the palm to the back of the hand between the middle and ring fingers (NB: left-handed people please refer to Appendix III); take it over the little and ring fingers, then once more from the palm to the back. This part of the operation creates just sufficient tension on the yarn to keep it taut during the crochet process. The yarn should now be brought over the middle and first fingers which should be spread to form a bridge. This allows the hook head to dip easily into the triangular space formed by the two fingers and the yarn (*diagram 2*). The hook then slides under the yarn and catches the thread almost involuntarily.

Diagram 2

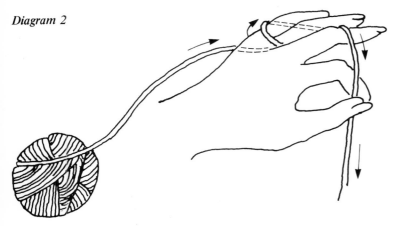

The actual crochet fabric being made is held and guided by the first finger and the thumb. This latter sometimes causes difficulty, but if you can remember to keep the first finger slightly straightened, and use a similarly straightened thumb to act as a pincer, the actual crochet work should lie between them in such a way that the tops of the stitches are showing and are readily accessible to the hook.

It should be reiterated that the holding of the yarn and work as shown here is only one method of doing so, albeit one that has proved to be successful for quite a large number of people. Should you have a different method that works well, do not attempt to change it.

SLIP KNOT

Unless there is a loop on the hook it is not possible to perform the action required to make a piece of crochet fabric. The loop is placed on the hook before any other process is undertaken. This means that because it is actually on the hook before commencing a stitch construction *it is not counted as a stitch*. It is purely the loop that makes the process of crochet possible. No matter how complicated a stitch operation is, before the stitch is constructed and when the stitch has been made, there will only be one single loop on the hook.

To avoid wasting yarn the best way to put a loop on the hook is to make a slip knot. This enables work to be pulled back entirely free of any wasted ends. To make a slip knot:

a cross the end of a ball of yarn over the main length coming from the ball, and form a loop (*diagram 3*);

b make sure there is sufficient yarn in the tail end to allow it to be taken over the thread coming from the ball, down behind the loop just made and then protrude below the loop by approximately 5cm (2in);

c insert the hook under this back thread from right to left and at the same time ensure the hook lies over both sides of the loop;

d first tighten the slip knot itself by gripping the 5cm (2in) length of yarn together with the thread from the ball and pulling the hook away from the knot. At this stage the knot rarely fits snugly around the stem of the hook. For this to happen pull the two strands of yarn coming out of the actual knot, away from each other. The knot will then tighten and will circle the stem of the hook snugly.

Diagram 3

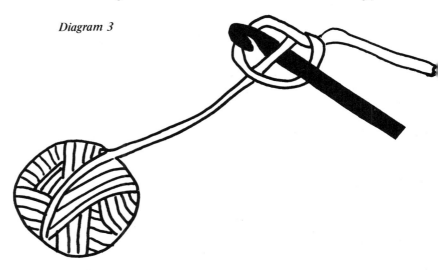

HOOK INSERTION

Unless you are following a printed pattern or attempting to carry out instructions given by someone else, the place where you insert the hook into the work is entirely a matter of choice. However, if you wish the final piece of crochet to have some sort of uniformity in its overall appearance, it is advisable to know what you are actually doing when you commence work and keep to that format for the rest of the article. It is not really important where you insert the hook into the work as long as you achieve a piece of crochet that is acceptable both in shape and appearance, as well as being of a suitable type of fabric for the job it is intended to do.

When following an instruction, be it a commercial crochet pattern, a process or suggestion given in this book, or in fact any other form of crochet directive, always insert the hook under *two* threads unless told to do otherwise (*diagram 4*). What happens when you choose another method of hook insertion will be gone into more fully in Chapters IV and V.

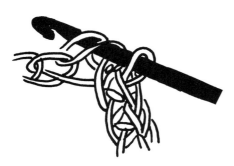

Diagram 4

BREAKING OFF YARN

When a piece of crochet has been completed it is time to break off the yarn. Those conversant with such crafts as knitting and macramé have no problem with the instruction 'break off yarn', but having seen work spoilt because of lack of knowledge on how to break off the yarn, I make no apologies for its inclusion here.

After the final stitch has been worked, break the yarn away from the main ball leaving a 15-25cm (6-10in) end. Remove the hook from the last loop still remaining and pull the yarn up through this loop. Slide the finger and thumb of the right hand down the 15-25cm (6-10in) end and at the same time pull the end firmly with the left hand. This produces a knot at the end of the work and leaves a piece of yarn sufficiently long to be threaded into a needle and invisibly darned into the work.

MIXING YARNS

It is no longer necessary to keep to the same type of yarn throughout when making an article. In the past a major drawback to mixing yarns of different fibre content has been the problem of laundering. With the advent of cold water washes it is now possible to mix different fibres as well as different textures which gives the crochet worker enormous scope. Follow the instructions given by the manufacturer and all will be well. Do not hesitate to use a washing machine if it is of the kind recommended, but *do* finish the drying process with the article lying flat.

JOINING YARNS

There are a number of different ways of joining yarn and as long as the method used withstands wear and laundering, cannot be seen, and cannot be found quickly by feel, then it is a good join.

The join which is the least bother to make, and at the same time is suitable for the majority of crochet fabrics, is to work the stitch to the point where the old yarn is collected and drawn through to the front of the work, after the hook has been inserted into the row below; leave this end and finish the stitch with the new ball of yarn (*diagram 5*). The two ends are now lying on top of the previous row and can be worked over until the ends disappear. In a firm fabric the only other precaution to take is to have the ends different lengths so that they chamfer down inside the stitches. If the stitches are of a loose structure because they have been worked on a large hook, or

Diagram 5

if the join is made in a lacy pattern, it will be necessary to hook the two ends through the back loop of each stitch until the whole of the ends have been twisted in. When joining with very thick yarn leave only one end to be worked over when the join occurs, the other end should then be lifted to the top of the stitch and worked over on the next row. If the yarn being used is extremely slippery, as in the case of rayon, it will be necessary discreetly to place a small flat knot at the base of the stitch where the joining has occurred, before working over the ends. As a further precaution, a drop of heat and water resistant glue can be put on a pin and inserted down the stitch where the join and the ends are.

JOINING IN A DIFFERENT COLOUR

The best method of incorporating a new yarn of a different colour is to join it into the work one stage before it is needed. If this is not done the old colour will drag into the base of the first stitch of the new colour. To join in a new colour at the beginning of a row, when working in stripes for example, crochet the row in the old colour until the last stitch is reached. Work the last stitch until two loops remain on the hook (*diagram 6*) and complete this stitch with the new colour. Make the turning chain in the new colour and proceed as normal.

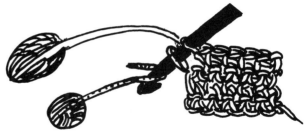

Diagram 6

Should the colour want changing in the middle of a row, again work the last stitch in the old colour until two loops remain, join the new colour in through these two loops but leave the end free at the top of the stitch. The end of the old colour can be worked over as described earlier, the end of the new colour can either be darned in with a needle or worked over on the row coming back, as long as the colour does not show through on the right side of the work. This can happen if the stitch structure is loose or the contrasting colour is very strong.

TENSION (GAUGE)

To find the tension (gauge) of the crochet fabric, first work a piece not less than 10cm (4in) square to enable the centre 5cm (2in) to be measured (*diagram 7*). The first two rows and foundation chain should be totally excluded from the measured 5cm (2in) square as tautness or frilling may occur until the pattern becomes familiar. In fact, if the pattern is a troublesome one, work one piece to ensure the texture and design are coming out correctly and then work a second piece to measure the tension (gauge). Always smooth crochet

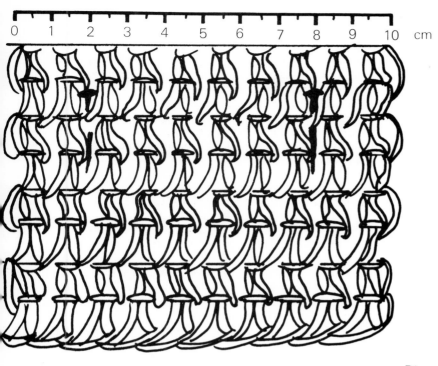

Diagram 7

away from the foundation chain, i.e. lengthways and *not* width-ways which is the usual procedure for other fabrics.

Before measuring, it is important that the crochet sample is put on a smooth surface so that the fibres of the yarn do not cling. The surface should also be flat as any curvature will alter the accuracy of the measurements. Measure the centre portion of the above diagram.

If there are too few stitches to 5cm (2in) the tension is too loose and it is necessary to use a smaller hook and once again make a tension (gauge) square with the new hook size. If there are too many stitches to 5cm (2in) the tension (gauge) is too tight and it is necessary to use a larger hook and make another tension (gauge) square. If there are exactly the number of stitches stated proceed to crochet the pattern. If the tension (gauge) is out by only half a stitch in a 5cm (2in) square the finished article can be anywhere from 2-8cm (½-3in) too small or too large.

ROWS

Certain rows are given names which can be confusing to someone new to the craft. A 'foundation row' is the row worked into the foundation — the initial — chain.

The very first row of crochet is often not the same as the rest of the work. For example, you work into the '4th chain from hook' when making trebles, but on the following row you work into the 'next stitch'. It is for this reason that patterns are frequently written with a foundation row, and are then followed by a pattern row or rows. Once the foundation row has been worked it is not used again except when starting another section of the article.

15

A 'pattern row' is the row that will be repeated throughout the work. There may be only one row and this will be referred to as the pattern row. Some patterns consist of more than one row and these will be written: 1st patt row, 2nd patt row, etc.

ABBREVIATIONS

Different designers and certainly different countries use different words to describe the same stitch or process. Therefore it is important to read the abbreviations in the pattern before commencing to crochet. A list of abbreviations for the United Kingdom and the United States are given at the beginning of this book. The international symbols are given in Appendix I, as are the hook sizes.

READING A PATTERN

The patterns given in the following chapters contain instructions and points to look out for that are not normally included. Appendix II covers patterns in more detail, so if there is still something in the reading of a pattern that causes you confusion you may find the answer there.

II Chain and Slipstitch

SECTION A

CHAIN (ch): no turning chain required
To make a chain, first put a slip knot on the hook. Place the yarn over the hook (yoh) by dipping the hook head under the strand of yarn lying between the middle and index fingers of the left hand. The yarn will automatically catch in the barbed part of the hook head and can then be drawn through the loop (lp) of the slip knot already on the hook, (*diagram 8*). Do make sure that the smooth part of the hook head is uppermost so that the yarn caught in the barb can slide through the loop on the hook — one chain made.

Continue in this manner until a sufficient number of chains has been made. Remember not to count the loop round the hook as this is the initial slip knot, only the chains below.

Chains are used for:

a Foundation chain. This is a length of chain determined by the number of stitches to be used in the fabric being made. Each chain represents a stitch after taking away the turning chain (see below)

b Turning chains. A turning chain is made at the end of each row to

Diagram 8

lift the crochet hook to the top of the next row to be made. (NB: The crochet hook 'sits' on top of the row being worked and therefore has to be raised to this level of the next row before proceeding.)
c To link small solid pattern pieces of crochet to each other in a lacy crochet fabric.

SLIP STITCH (ss [sl st]): no turning chain required
A slip stitch is a chain that is anchored to a stitch. There is no height to a slip stitch. To make a ss (sl st), insert the hook into the work picking up 2 strands of yarn unless the pattern tells you differently, yoh, draw the yarn through the place where the hook is inserted and through the lp already on the hook (*diagram 9*) — one slip stitch made. Its main uses are:
a To join rows together to make rounds when working circles for motifs, doilies, hats, etc.
b To join rows together to make tubes when making seamless sleeves, trouser legs, gloves, etc.
c To carry the yarn over stitches which no longer need to be worked e.g. at the beginning of a decrease row when it is necessary to reduce more than two stitches at a time. By working a slip stitch into each stitch, no extra depth has been added to the work and each stitch retains the chain formation at the top which is needed for future crochet processes.
d As a connecting stitch in some crochet fabric patterns.

Diagram 9

SECTION B

To appreciate the versatility of crochet one has to experiment with various hook sizes and alternative types of yarn. Although the stitch pattern is not altered, the crochet fabric being produced will look and feel quite different just by changing the size of hook. The smaller the hook, the firmer the fabric; conversely with a larger hook the crochet fabric will be more open and feel softer. In a similar way the fabric will alter by changing the type and thickness of yarn even though the stitch pattern and hook size remain the same. Thus, a thicker yarn will result in a stiffer crochet fabric and a thinner yarn will become looser and more pliable.

The only way to understand how yarns, hooks and stitch patterns react with one another is to try for yourself. Initially try three hook sizes: 2.50mm (B); 5.00mm (H); and a 10.00mm (15 wood). Use these three hook sizes to make a chain of 30-40 stitches in each of the following five types of yarn.
a 20s crochet cotton
b a plain smooth acrylic yarn of sweater thickness (DK [worsted])
c pure wool Aran
d a thin fluffy yarn such as a mohair mixture
e a thick bouclé or slub yarn

You could have difficulty to begin with in keeping a standard tension (gauge), and one way to overcome the problem is to hold your hook closer to the barbed head when working with the fine steel hooks for cotton, sizes 0.60-2.00mm (5-14) and when using the larger hooks sizes 7.00-15.00mm (K-wood 15) hold the hook very low down the stem away from the head. This enables the loops to be pushed well down past the tapering section leading into the barb, thus ensuring the loops are made to the correct circumference.

SECTION C

Now that you can manipulate your hook and yarn sufficiently to produce a slip knot, chain and slipstitch you may like to try the following overtop pattern, which has been designed in such a way that a slightly incorrect tension (gauge) will not matter *too* much. Before you begin please note carefully the following points:

a Do check the tension (gauge) by making a small piece using the correct hook and the yarn with which you intend to make the garment. Besides finding out whether or not you have a correct tension, you will also get the feel of the work and become familiar with the stitch pattern. Work a piece commencing with 29 chain which will give you six loops and do at least six rows. It is important that your chains are not too uneven as they will show. Most beginners have a tendency to crochet chains tightly. Please make sure that your chains are *loosely* worked.

b In all patterns, you pick up two strands of yarn when inserting your hook unless it states differently, so please note that in this particular pattern you are told to pick up only *one* strand.

c There is no right or wrong side to crochet until you make it have a right or wrong side. In this pattern, that means the work is reversible until after the seams are made.

d Joining in a new ball of yarn is more difficult with an open pattern. To get a neat join in this overtop, first finish with a ss (sl st). Make 1 ch and pull the end through this ch as though completing the work. Insert the hook in the 5 ch sp just made close to the final ss (sl st), pull yarn through to right side. Work 1 ch with 2 threads, 4 ch with the single main thread, tie a reef knot with the 2 short ends and loosely darn these in.

e Where the pattern says '1 ss (sl st) in ch sp' it means inserting the hook into the hole or loops made by the five chains of the previous row. However, where the pattern says '1 ss (sl st) in next ch' it means inserting the hook into the actual chain stitch.

f When making the extensions for the sleeves which give a T-shape it is important that they are both added on the same row at the same time, or one sleeve will be narrower than the other.

g The foundation row has to stretch over the upper part of the hips. If this is crocheted too tightly it will not do this.

h Counting the rows is easier, particularly in this pattern, if you count the diamonds and multiply by two, as two rows make one diamond (*figure 1*).

i When putting the two pieces together for joining, it is simpler if the 6 chain loops made for the beginning of the row are placed together. It is important that the slip stitches made during the joining are worked very loosely indeed or the seams will be tight, pucker and not give a straight line on the hips.

OVERTOP (Colour plate I)

Materials: 160g [190g; 220g] of a soft 4-ply such as Falcon Llama, Patons Kismet, (fine alpaca, or fine mohair mixture), a Baby 4-ply (Baby knit)
4.00mm (F) hook

Measurement: To fit bust sizes 81-86 [92-97; 102-107] cm (32-34 [36-38; 40-42] in)

Tension (gauge): 3 loops to approx. 3.5cm (2½in)

Main piece (2 alike)
With 4.00mm (F) hook make 85 [93; 101] ch.
Foundation row: 1 ss (sl st) in 9th ch from hook picking up 1 strand only, *5 ch, miss 3 ch, 1 ss (sl st) in top of next ch, rep from * to end (20 [22; 24] ch lps made). 6 ch, turn.
Patt row: *1 ss (sl st) in ch sp, 5 ch, rep from * to last sp, 1 ss (sl st) in top of 3rd ch of 6 ch rem, 6 ch, turn.
Rep patt row 32 times to give a length of approx 30cm (12in) but omit the 6 ch to turn on the last row (*figure 1*).

Sleeve extensions
Without turning work make 38 ch for one underarm seam and leave the last lp in a safety pin.
     With a new ball of yarn, insert the hook into the 3rd ch of the end lp at the rh side of the same row of the work, make 32 ch with this for the other underarm seam. Break off this new yarn.
Next row: With the yarn that is still attached, remove safety pin, turn work, 1 ss (sl st) in top of 9th ch, *5 ch, miss 3 ch, 1 ss (sl st) in top of next ch, rep from * 6 times, **5 ch, 1 ss (sl st) in next ch sp, rep from ** 18 times, 5 ch, 1 ss (sl st) in place where the extension yarn was joined in, ***5 ch, miss 3 ch, 1 ss (sl st) in top of next ch, rep from *** 7 times, 6 ch, turn.
     Work a further 25 rows patt. Break off yarn.

Shoulder join
Put the two pieces of work tog. Connect the end 13 lps on each side leaving the centre 10 lps free for neck. A good join is to sew 3 times into centre ch of lp on both pieces, thread yarn down to a ss (sl st) on one piece, make a back st in ss (sl st) and thread yarn up to centre of next ch lp.

Underarm and side seams
Starting at sleeve edge, loosely ss (sl st) the underarm foundation ch and side chs tog, matching patt and working into every st.

Edges
Sleeves: With rs facing join yarn at cuff edge to underarm seam, *5 ch, ss (sl st) in same place as ss (sl st) on turning ch, * rep from * all round cuff edge. Fasten off. (It does not really matter how or where you insert the hook as long as you do it in the same manner all round the sleeve edge.)
Base: With rs facing join yarn to a side seam, *5 ch, 1 ss (sl st) in same place as ss (sl st) of foundation row, rep from * round both

Figure 1 Close up of stitch pattern of overtop using chains and slip stitches

sides, fasten off. Should you wish to lengthen the sleeves or body extra rows can be worked at this point.

Four strands of the yarn in which the overtop is made can be worked together and a chain crocheted long enough to thread through the loops at waist level. Tie at the side.

SECTION D

The pattern for the overtop can be adapted in the following ways.

a Omit the sleeve extensions. This will give a tabard design (less yarn required).

b Work in a 4-ply glitter yarn as an evening blouse.

c Have a shorter sleeve by making 22 ch instead of 38 ch at the end of the row and 16 ch instead of 32 ch with the separate piece of yarn at the beginning of the row.

d A longer sleeve is achieved by making 58 ch instead of 38 ch at the end of the row and 16 ch instead of 32 ch with the separate piece of yarn at the beginning of the row.

e Work two different balls of 2-ply yarn together to give a tweed effect.

f Work rows 6-12 in a contrast colour. Also work the last six rows along sleeves and neck piece in contrast colour. The border can be in either the main shade or the contrast.

Once the stitch pattern can be made, keeping the edges straight, you can try to work out patterns for the following for yourself.

  i a fine mohair or chenille stole using a thin mohair or thin chenille.
 ii a string shopping bag or beach bag.
iii a silk or acrylic scarf using a lightweight yarn.
 iv garden nets in fine fishing line.
  v a net curtain using 10s cotton.

The only thing to remember is that the foundation chain should be divisible by four with one extra chain for anchoring the last slip stitch into. If you use this calculation and always go into the ninth chain at the start of the foundation row, your pattern will work out accurately.

WHAT IS DESIGN?

The easiest introduction to crochet design is to use a pattern that has already had the calculations for yarn, hook and stitches worked out by someone else and then change it to give it an individual touch. This is the essence of the first part of the D sections throughout this book. They give alternative suggestions for using the shape, or stitch pattern, or yarn, written in the original pattern design. These suggestions are not exhaustive, they simply nudge the mind to think in other directions. The rest is up to you.

III Double Crochet

SECTION A

DOUBLE CROCHET (single crochet) (dc [sc]): 1 chain to turn.
To make a dc (sc) st, insert the hook into the work from front to back picking up 2 strands of the st, yoh and draw through to the front of the work. This gives 2 lps on the hook. Yoh, and draw this through the 2 lps on the hook — 1 dc (sc) made (*diagram 10*).

The stitches in crochet vary in height. A double crochet (single crochet) is a short stitch. As the crochet hook sits on top of the row being worked it is necessary at the start of the row to lift the hook up to the right height. To do this turning chains have to be made, and the number of chains required depends upon the height of the row to be worked next. In this chapter all the rows will be made of double crochet (single crochet) therefore all rows will start with one chain. This chain counts as a stitch and is the first stitch of the row.

To make a piece of dc (sc) fabric with straight sides, commence with a foundation ch. The number of sts in the foundation ch should equal the number of dc (sc) sts for the crochet fabric, plus one ch. The 1st dc (sc) of the 1st row is worked into the 3rd ch from the hook, pick up 2 threads of the ch when inserting the hook into the work (*diagram 10a*). A dc (sc) is then made in each ch until all the sts of the foundation ch have been worked into. Before turning to do the 2nd row, make 1 ch. Turn the work away from you, into the palm of the hand. It must be stressed that the 1 ch made just before turning the work is the 1st st of the row. Now insert the hook into the 2nd st of the row just made, remembering that the lp on the hook is not counted and once again picking up the two strands of the st. Continue working 1 dc (sc) into each st to the end of the row. The very last st of a dc (sc) row is worked into the turning ch.

Newcomers to working dc (sc) often find difficulty in keeping the correct number of stitches throughout. Frequently this is because the turning chain of the row below has not always been used. A good phrase to think about is 'work to the last hole and then put 1 dc (sc) in the "knot" '.

To count dc (sc) sts count the ch lps lying on the top of the sts and remember the turning ch is counted as 1 st. It is easier to count dc (sc) rows two at a time as 2 dc (sc) rows together form what appear to be parallel lines with dashes between (*figure 2*).

TO INCREASE (inc)
Increasing in crochet is easy as you simply put two stitches where you normally put one.

a at the beginning of a row: make 1 dc (sc) into the 1st st alongside the turning ch. As the turning ch is 1 st, another st put at its base means an increase of 1 st.

b at the end of the row: put 2 dc (sc) sts into the 'knot' or turning ch.

c to increase a large number of sts at once: make a length of ch and work into it.

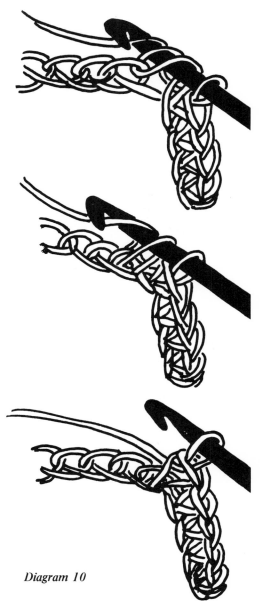

Diagram 10

Figure 2 *Piece of double crochet (single crochet) with hook changes every four rows* **a** *2.00mm (cotton 4),* **b** *300mm (C),* **c** *4.00mm (F),* **d** *5.00mm (H),* **e** *600mm (I),* **f** *7.00mm (K),* **g** *8.0mm (wood 12)* **h** *9.00mm (wood 15),* **i** *10.00mm*

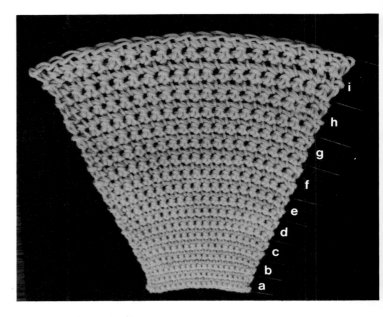

TO DECREASE (dec)

a **at the beginning of a row**: the turning ch should have been made and the work turned. Insert hook into 2nd st of row, yoh, draw lp through, insert hook into 3rd st of row below, yoh, draw lp through (3 lps on hook), yoh, draw through all 3 lps. There is now 1 ch top over 2 dc (sc) sts — one decrease made.

b **at the end of the row**: insert the hook into the last hole, i.e. next to last st, draw through to front of work and leave lp on hook, now insert hook into the 'knot', i.e. last st, yoh, draw through to front of work (3 lps on hook), yoh, draw through all 3 lps.

c **to decrease by a large number of stitches:**

at the beginning of a row: ss (ss st) across the number of sts to be missed, lift the crochet hook with a turning ch ready to continue with dc (sc).

at the end of the row: simply stop and leave the sts unworked, make a turning ch, turn work and proceed as usual.

Before going further it is advisable to do small practice pieces of the three processes outlined above using an aran thickness of wool and a 5.00mm (H) hook. This will show the structure of the stitch clearly and make the following practice pieces simpler to handle for a learner.

a a straight sided piece of dc (sc) fabric

b a piece of dc (sc) fabric with inc sides gaining 1 st at either end of each row.

c a piece of dc (sc) fabric with dec sides, losing 1 st at either end of each row.

SECTION B

As explained in Chapter II, Section B, the only way to understand how a stitch looks and reacts to different hook sizes (*figure 2*) and/ or different yarns, is actually to work a piece for yourself. The following suggestions produce interesting results. Use

a a plain smooth acrylic yarn of sweater thickness, e.g. DK (worsted)
b pure new wool — aran type
c a thin fluffy yarn such as a fine mohair mixture
d a thick bouclé or slub yarn omitting hook size 2.50mm (B) and in each of the above yarns work a square of dc (sc) with:

  i 21 ch giving 20 sts on a 2.50mm (B) hook
 ii 15 ch giving 14 sts on a 5.00mm (H) hook
iii 11 ch giving 10 sts on a 10.00mm (wool 15) hook
 Also work squares of dc (sc) in 20s cotton:
a on a 1.00mm (cotton 6) hook and
b on a 2.00mm (cotton 1) hook.

As well as changing the hook size and/or yarn to give a different look and a different feel to a crochet fabric, it is also possible to change the angle of insertion of the hook. It is important to remember that unless the pattern gives alternative instructions the hook should be inserted under the two strands lying on the top of the stitch being worked into.

DOUBLE CROCHET (SINGLE CROCHET) RIB

A ridged effect with an elasticated texture can be obtained by inserting the hook under the back loop of each double crochet (single crochet) stitch on every row after the foundation row. (The foundation row being the row worked into the initial length of chain). A narrow strip of this stitch can be used for a welt if worked sideways. It also has a pleasing textured finish which enables it to be used as a straight fabric in its own right (see pattern for suit on p.26). However, in this method of working double crochet (single crochet) it is a little more difficult to keep the sides straight.

To help overcome this, it is suggested that in this particular pattern only, the work is turned towards you away from the palm, having already worked the one turning chain first. Insert the hook into the back lp of the 3rd st down counting the turning ch as the 1st st (*diagram 11*). Work 1 dc (sc) into the back lp of each st to the end. The very last st is worked into the back of the knot, i.e. the back of the turning ch.

Diagram 11

CRAB STITCH (cr st)

There are many names for this stitch which is really a double crochet (single crochet) worked backwards, i.e. worked from left to right instead of from right to left. It is known as: rope stitch, rope edge, Russian stitch, corded edge, reversed double crochet (single crochet) and shrimp stitch, as well as crab stitch.

Diagram 12

This stitch is nearly always used as an edging and by the time you come to work it there will be a right side to the crochet either because one side looks neater or because of shaping, so to work this version of double crochet (single crochet) have the rs facing. Insert the hook into the next st on the right picking up 2 strands. Collect the yarn from the ball by dropping the hook head onto the thread rather than trying to put yoh in the normal manner (*diagram 12*). Now bring this thread through to the front of the work tilting the hook upwards to ensure there are 2 lps on the hook. (NB: at this stage it is easy to pull the yarn straight through all lps which would give you a reversed ss (sl st) and not a reversed dc (sc). Bring the hook back into the normal working position, yoh, draw through 2 lps on the hook — one crab stitch made.

In this publication crab stitch is used mainly as an edging to remove the chain stitch look of the last row of stitches. It is also used as a joining stitch, and is particularly useful if two pieces of crochet fabric are to be joined together on the right side as it gives a textured effect. To include crab stitch as part of a piece of crochet fabric results in a prominent ridge effect and is not included here. It is therefore suggested that a sample piece of double crochet (single crochet) be worked using aran yarn and a 5.00mm (H) hook and going into the back loop of the stitch only. Make the very last row a crab stitch edge.

SECTION C

SCARF/CRAVAT WITH RING (*figure 3*)

If you have made sample pieces of dc (sc) with straight sides, dc (sc) with incs and dc (sc) with decs, you can make this scarf with the diamond-shaped end. You may not, as yet, feel confident to inc and/or dec in which case start with 19 ch to make 18 dc (sc) and proceed from * on the pattern. The last few rows are dc (sc) worked into the back lp only for greater elasticity as described in Section B. This can however be worked straight in the normal way if wished.

Materials
1 x 50g ball Patons Beehive Double Knitting (worsted)
4.00mm (F) hook

Tension (gauge)
10 sts to 6cm (4 sts to 1in)
2 rows to 1cm (10 rows to 2in)

To make
3 ch.
Row 1 1 dc (sc) in first ch made, 1 ch, turn.
Row 2 1 dc (sc) at base of turning ch (1 dc [sc] inc made) 1 dc (sc), 1 ch, turn.
Row 3 1 dc (sc) inc, 2 dc (sc), 1 ch, turn.
Row 4 1 dc (sc) inc, 3 dc (sc), 1 ch, turn, (5 sts).
Continue inc in the 1st st until there are 23 sts.
Row 24 1 dc (sc) inc, 20 dc (sc), dec 1 dc (sc) over the 2 sts rem (see p.22) 1 ch, turn, (23 sts).
Row 25 20 dc (sc), dec 1 dc (sc) over 2 sts rem, 1 ch, turn.

Figure 3 *Shaped cravat in double crochet (single crochet) using various techniques*

Plate 1   *Simple but versatile overtop using only a chain and slip stitch*

Plate 3   *Textured waistcoats. Only the stitch pattern is given, the choice of yarn is left to the individual so no two are alike*

Plate 2   *The peacock cloak uses a base of flecked mohair and acrylic in long trebles with raised treble (double crochet) spars. The 'eyes' of the peacock feathers are motifs worked in many stitches, using very fine lurex yarns. Each motif was then fringed and sewn into position*

Continue dec 1 st at the end of each row until there are 18 sts.
*Work 96 rows dc (sc) with straight sides.
Work 26 rows dc (sc) crocheting into the back lp only keeping straight sides. Fasten off.
Fold the last 26 rows in half and sew down to the last row of plain fabric. This latter forms a tube through which the pointed end of the scarf can be threaded.
Check all ends are invisibly fastened in.

SIX PANEL DAY SKIRT (*front cover*)

It is important to work a 15cm (6in) sample length on a 7.00mm (K) hook starting with 9 ch giving 8 dc (sc) and inc 1 st at the beg of every row, to check that the tension (gauge) is correct. It is also important that before you commence work on the skirt you feel completely confident in working both dc (sc) and in increasing. Chenille is one of the more expensive yarns, and although it does pull back it goes thinner each time it is re-used. To avoid this use two balls of the matching DK (worsted) together as one yarn, to work the sample. This should give you the same tension (gauge) as the Chenille but does not suffer the same ill-effects when pulled back. To join Chenille: leave an 8cm (3in) length and tie a knot at the base of the stitch using an 8cm (3in) length from the beginning of the new ball. Shred the velvety bits away from the two ends and oversew the remaining cotton-like core into the back of the work.
NB: Before completing the first skirt panel hang it pinned to a padded hanger for at least 48 hours whilst working the other panels. If the skirt is going to drop it will do so whilst hung up and before being worn.

Materials
5 [6; 6; 7] balls Sirdar Chenille
2 [2; 2; 2] balls Sirdar Majestic DK (worsted)
7.00mm (K) hook, 5.50mm (H) hook
Elastic to fit waist measurement 2.5cm (1in) wide
10cm (4in) zip (optional)

Measurement
To fit waist 66-72 [73-81; 82-88; 89-95] cm (26-28 [29-31; 32-34; 35-37] in)
Approx hip (as it is not a fitted skirt) 92 [99; 107; 114] cm (36 [39; 42; 45] in)

Tension (gauge)
15 sts to 18cm (7in)

Skirt panel (6 alike)
With 7.00mm (K) hook and Chenille make 10 [11; 12; 13] ch.
Row 1 1 dc (sc) in 3rd ch from hook, 1 dc (sc) to end, 1 ch, turn (9 [10; 11; 12] sts).
Row 2 dc (sc) to end, 1 ch, turn.
Row 3 1 dc (sc) in same place as turning ch (1 inc made), dc (sc) to end, 1 ch, turn, (10 [11; 12; 13] sts).
Rows 4 & 5 as row 2.
Row 6 As row 3 (11 [12; 13; 14] sts).

Continue in dc (sc) until 60 rows have been made increasing only on rows, 9, 12, 17, 22, 27, 34, 41, 52, (19 [20; 21; 22] sts). If necessary for extra length a further increase can be made on row 61. Break off yarn.

To join

After all panels have been hung for at least 3 days, place ws of 2 panels together. Working with 2 balls of DK (worsted) tog join one edge of the panels on rs with cr st. Repeat with the other panels until all 6 panels are connected. An opening for a 10cm (4in) zip can be left at the top of one seam if desired.

With rs facing work cr st round hem of skirt and round waist edge. Make a casing for the elastic as follows:

Using two balls of DK yarn (worsted) tog and a 5.50mm (H) hook, join to inside of a seam at waist edge.

*3 ch, ss (sl st) into back of a st 2 rows below and 2-3 sts along, 3 ch ss (sl st) into back of st 2-3 sts along at waist level. Rep from * until all the waist has been worked. Fasten off. Insert elastic into casing, securing it firmly at either side of the zip.

EDGE TO EDGE JACKET (*figure 4*)

It is recommended that you work at least four other articles before attempting this jacket. Although the instructions are for one size only, additional rows can be worked between † and †† to increase the size as there are no shoulder widths to be changed. Should the jacket be for a person with a thicker than average neck, extra rows can be worked at ‡.

Materials

13 x 50g balls Sirdar Majestic DK (worsted)
NB: This is a very economical yarn, you would possible require more of another brand.
2 balls Sirdar Chenille
8.00mm (wool 11) hook

Measurements

To fit bust size 84-92cm (33-36in)
Underarm sleeve seam 42cm (16½in)
Back length 56cm (22in)

Tension (gauge)

15 sts to 18cm (7in) worked over dc inserting hook under 2 strands.

To make

Beginning at sleeve edge with two balls DK (worsted) as one yarn and 8.00mm (wood 11) hook make 33 ch.
Row 1 1 dc (sc) in 3rd ch from hook, picking up only *1* strand of the st, 1 dc (sc) in each ch to end, 1 ch, turn, (32 sts).
Row 2 *1 dc (sc) in back lp of next st, rep from * to end, 1 ch, turn. Rep Row 2, 6 times.
Row 9 1 dc (sc) in back of first st (i.e. one used by the turning ch), *1 dc (sc) in back lp of next st, rep from * to end, 1 ch, turn, (33 sts).
Continue by working in back lps of sts throughout.
Inc as in row 9, on rows 10, 17, 18, 25, 26.

Figure 4 *Double crochet (single crochet) jacket with the main part crocheted into the back loop only*

Work row 2 twice.

Now work row 9, 8 times, (46 sts).

Continue the last row with 36 ch made loosely, remove hook and place a safety pin in the lp. Without turning work join two more DK (worsted) threads to top of turning ch at beg of same row.

Makes 35 ch loosely with these threads. Fasten off the new threads. Turn work.

Next row 1 dc (sc) in top of 3rd ch from hook, picking up 1 strand only, 1 dc (sc) in top of next 33 ch, 1 dc (sc) in back lp of next 46 sts, 1 dc (sc) in top of next 35 ch, (116 sts).

†Work row 2, 23 times.††

Next row 1 dc (sc) in back lp of next 53 sts, 1 ch, turn.

Work row 2, 11 times on these 54 sts.‡

Continue the last row by loosely making 63 ch.

Next row 1 dc (sc) in top of 3rd ch from hook, 1 dc (sc) in top of next 60 ch, 1 dc (sc) in back lp of each rem st to end.

†Work row 2, 23 times.†† Break off yarn. Turn work, and rejoin yarn to 36th st, 1 ch, 1 dc (sc) in back lp of next 45 sts, 1 ch, turn.

Dec row (yoh, insert into next st, draw yarn through to front) twice, yoh, draw through all 3 lps — one dec made. Dc (sc) to end, 1 ch, turn.

Work the dec row 7 times more, (38 sts).

Work row 2, twice.

(**Work 2 dec rows followed by row 2), 6 times. Rep from ** twice. Fasten off.

The work now consists of 2 sleeves, a back and 2 incomplete fronts.

Left front
Rejoin yarn to 13th st from neck * thus leaving 12 sts unworked.
Work as row 2 on the rem 50 sts for 6 rows, break off yarn.

Right front
Rejoin yarn to 13th st from neck. If only the top of the ch has been worked into as instructed there will be 2 lps left to work into now. Work into back of the rem ch lps as though it were an ordinary st. Work as left front from *.

Cuffs (2 alike)
Using chenille work 4 rows dc (sc) at cuff edge. Finish with 1 row cr st. Fasten off.

Front border
With rs facing, start at base of front edge with Chenille. Work 1 dc (sc) for each st and 1 dc (sc) for each row. Continue in this manner up the right front, round neck, down the left front, 1 ch, turn. It is possible that the front borders may not lie flat, in this case dec 3 or 4 times when putting in the 1st row of dc (sc). Work 3 rows dc (sc) putting 3 sts in the corner st of point at neck edge on each row, and dec 1 st at irregular intervals 3 times round the neck on each row, (NB: do not dec in the same place as previous row or you will not get a smooth curved neck). Complete with 1 row cr st.

SECTION D

IDEAS FOR SCARVES

The following is a selection of ways to make a scarf using the information given in Sections A and B.

a Using a single colour DK (worsted) yarn and 5.00mm (H) hook, work 15cm (6in) in dc (sc) inserting hook under 2 lps in the normal way, followed by 10cm (4in) in dc (sc) worked into back lp only, finishing with a block of plain dc (sc). So that all ways of using dc (sc) as shown above have been utilized, edge the scarf with cr st.

b Beg with 21 ch to give 20 dc (sc), use DK (worsted) yarn and a 4.50mm (G) hook, * inc 1 st at beg of next 10 rows, work 10 rows straight, dec 1 st at end of next 10 rows, work 10 rows straight, rep from * until scarf has reached required length.

c Using oddments of DK (worsted) yarn and a 5.00mm (H) hook make a random striped scarf with pointed ends. To do this proceed as given for the cravat pattern (p.24) until the scarf is almost the required length. Complete by inc 1 st at beg of the next 5 rows. Work the next row with an inc at the beg of the row and a dec at the end. Then dec 1 st at end of each row until no sts rem.

d An alternative to (c) is to make the colours in the scarf the same for both halves. This is achieved by working both halves at the same time in 2 separate pieces and joining the scarf at the centre back.

e If a mohair yarn, 7.00mm (K) hook and 17 ch for 16 dc (sc) is used, a warm lightweight scarf will result.

VARIATIONS ON THE SKIRT PATTERN

a The skirt can be made by using two balls of DK (worsted) yarn as one working thread throughout.

b The DK (worsted) yarn can be of a contrast colour to the Chenille.

c A two-coloured skirt can be achieved by working alternate panels in a contrast.

d Instead of inc, make rectangular strips of Chenille the length of the skirt and to fit the waist measure. Triangles of the DK (worsted) yarn can then be made to insert between the strips, giving the necessary fullness at hips and hem.

e Using a contrast yarn work two or more panels with surface crochet.

VARIATIONS FOR THE JACKET PATTERN

a Work in either all Chenille or all DK (worsted) (still using the two DK [worsted] balls tog as one yarn).

b Use a contrast colour for dc (sc) bands and cr st edge.

c For a 'tweed' effect work with two different colours of DK (worsted) yarn using just one of the colours for the Chenille bands.

d Work broader bands at the front and include buttonholes down one side. Buttonholes are made by missing 1 st and replacing the st with a ch (see p.90).

e For a very slimming effect work front and neck bands in two colours (or two tones of one colour) alternating the colours on each row.

NB: It is not advisable with this pattern to add patch pockets.

FIRST STEPS IN DESIGN

During your experiments with yarns and hook sizes you may have had an idea that you might like to try, in some article of clothing. Initially avoid curves, but with the information on increasing and decreasing given above any angular shape should be within your grasp. A way of tackling your own design is suggested here:

a Make a tension (gauge) square and *accurately* measure the number of stitches and rows (see p. 15). It is better to do two tension (gauge) squares when designing. The first piece enables you to come to terms with the yarn, hook and stitches. The second piece gives a more accurate tension (gauge) measurement.

b Draw to size on a large piece of paper the shape to be crocheted, as an easy-to-check aid.

c Decide in which direction the work is to proceed, e.g. up, sideways, down, in panels, etc.

d Calculate the number of stitches required for the first row of each shape to be crocheted.

e Find the answers to any problems concerning corners, increasing/decreasing, stitch pattern etc. on spare yarn before commencing the article, particularly if using a textured yarn.

f Make the foundation chain (plus one for double crochet [single crochet]) and begin.

g After a few rows, recheck the tension (gauge) as it sometimes alters when a pattern becomes familiar.

IV Trebles

SECTION A

TREBLES (DOUBLE CROCHET) (tr [dc]): 3 chain to turn

To make a tr (dc) st, yoh, and insert hook into work picking up two strands of the st, yoh and draw this through to the front of the work. This gives 3 lps on the hook, yoh again and draw the thread in the hook head through the first 2 lps thus leaving 2 lps still on the hook, place yoh once more and draw through remaining 2 lps — one treble (double crochet) made (*diagram 13*).

The height of a treble (double crochet) is twice that of a double crochet (single crochet). The number of turning chains given for a treble (double crochet) is three, and for most people this is the right number of turning chains to use. However, try a sample piece of treble (double crochet) and see whether the turning chain is exactly the height of the stitches or whether it leaves a hole. If there is an obvious hole use only two chains to turn, and adjust any patterns you work accordingly. *Do not* make this adjustment to the foundation row.

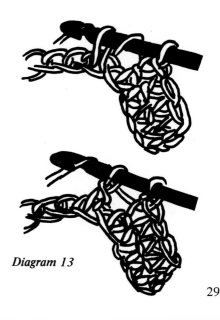

Diagram 13

29

Figure 5a *trebles (double crochet)*

To make a piece of tr (dc) fabric with straight sides commence with a foundation ch containing 2 chs more than the number of sts required. Work 1st tr (dc) into 4th ch from hook picking up 2 strands of the ch as previously explained (p. 29). Continue working 1 tr (dc) in each st to the end of the foundation ch. Make 3 ch before turning. These chains count as the first st of the row. Count 4 ch tops (3 for turning and 1 st) and work a tr (dc) in next st. Work 1 tr (dc) into each tr (dc) picking up 2 strands and also work 1 tr (dc) into top of the 3 turning ch of the row below. If the work has been turned into the palm of the hand as shown in diagram 11 the flat side of the turning ch will be facing, thus making it easier for the hook to be inserted.

The easiest way to count tr (dc) sts is to count the stems with the 3 chs at the beginning of a row equalling one 'stem'. Because tr (dc) sts are taller than dc (sc) sts they are easier to count. The main problem when counting rows of tr (dc) arises from the fact that the sts do not sit exactly on top of each other as they do say, in knitting, so familiarize yourself with the look of the treble (dc) fabric right from the start then counting the rows will come naturally (*figure 5a*).

TO INCREASE
a at the beginning of a row: make 1 tr (dc) into st belonging to the turning ch
b at the end of the row: put 2 tr (dc) into top of turning ch of row below thus making an extra st.
c to increase by a large number of sts:
at beginning of a row: work a length of ch the number of sts required plus 2 turning ch.
at the end of the row: before turning, attach another piece of yarn to top of turning ch of row just worked and make a length of ch the number of sts required for the inc as worked in the overtop see (p. 19).

TO DECREASE
a at the beginning of a row: the turning ch should have been made and the work turned. *Yoh, insert hook into next st, yoh, draw lp to front, yoh, draw through 2 lps on hook leaving 2 lps still on hook, yoh, insert hook into next st, yoh, and draw through to front (4 lps on hook), yoh, draw through 1st 2 lps, yoh, draw through rem 3 lps. There is now only 1 ch top over the 2 sts just worked, showing 1 dec has been made, **
b at the end of the row: work along the row until 2 sts rem i.e. 1 tr (dc) and the 3 ch to turn of the row below. Work these 2 sts as from * to ** given in (**a**) above. There is now only 1 ch top over the 2 sts just worked showing 1 dec has been made, (*diagram 14*).
c to decrease by a large number of sts:
at the beginning of a row: ss (sl st) across the number of sts no longer required, work 3 ch to raise the hook to the right height and proceed across the work as usual making sure the pattern is kept.
at the end of the row: just leave the sts to be decreased unworked. Make 3 ch, turn work, and proceed in pattern as usual.

Using the above information make a practice piece of treble (double crochet) using an aran thickness of wool and a 5.00mm (H) hook. This gives a tension (gauge) of 3 sts to 2cm (4in) and 2 rows to 3cm ($1^3/_8$ in). Work on a foundation ch of not less than 17 which

2nd stitch

1st stitch

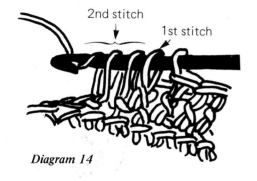

Diagram 14

gives 15 sts, if first tr (dc) is put in 4th ch from hook. Make a treble (double crochet) fabric with straight sides and work this until you are confident that the tension (gauge) is even.

A common error when first working trebles (double crochet) is to insert the hook into the stitch in a horizontal position. This pulls the yarn away from the top of the row below and forms a large loop, thus giving a loose tension (gauge). The loop initially on the hook, the yarn wrapped round the hook before insertion into the stitch, and the loop pulled through to the front, should all sit snugly round the stem of the hook to give an accurate tension (gauge). If any of these loops are in the narrowed section of the hook head the tension (gauge) will be tight.

Once the trebles (double crochet) being worked are of an even tension (gauge) with straight sides, work a few rows of increasing followed by a few rows of decreasing, to get the feel and look of the stitches.

SECTION B

To see how trebles (double crochet) look with different types of yarn and different hook sizes repeat the suggestions made for double crochet (single crochet) (see p. 23). Follow this by making the stitch patterns below using aran wool and a 5.00mm (H) hook which will give a different appearance to a treble (double crochet) fabric.

An open effect can be achieved by inserting the hook between the stems of the treble (double crochet), that is under three strands. This pushes the trebles (double crochet) sideways so causing the fabric to be shorter and wider than a piece of treble (double crochet) crocheted in the usual way by inserting the hook under two strands.

Alternatively, a stitch can be missed and after the next stitch has been worked into, the space can be filled in to give crossed trebles (double crochet), i.e. work the stitches in the following order: 1 3 2 5 4 7 6 9 8 etc. finishing with a straight treble (double crochet) stitch.

Another way to change the appearance of a piece of treble (double crochet) fabric is to put more than one stitch together in a group and then miss stitches so that there is no increasing. The 'V' stitch pattern does this.

Lacy fabrics can be produced by working a chain and then missing a stitch followed by a treble (double crochet) as in the crochet netting below.

TREBLES (DOUBLE CROCHET) BETWEEN TREBLES (DOUBLE CROCHET)

Because this fabric spreads sideways, pulling can be avoided by working the foundation chain on a size larger hook. Work the last two chains on the right size hook.

Foundation row 1 tr (dc) in 4th ch from hook, 1 tr (dc) in ch to end, 3 ch to turn.

Patt row 1 tr (dc) in sp between the end and the next to the end tr (dc) of the row below. (i.e. insert the hook in the large sp and pick up 3 strands and not in the small sp at the top of the tr [dc] which picks up 2 strands.) *1 tr (dc) in sp between trs (dcs), rep from * to end. (Do not work in the turning ch, just between ch and tr [dc], 3 ch, turn) (*figure 5b*).

Figure 5b *trebles (double crochet worked between trebles (double crochet)*

b

c

d

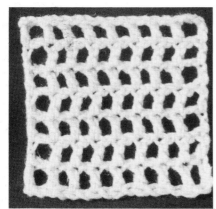

e

Figure 5c 'V' sts
Figure 5d crossed trebles (double crochet)
Figure 5e net of treble (double crochet) 1 chain

'V' STITCH

As with the pattern above, the hook is being inserted into the space between the treble (double crochet) stitches. Because every other chain is missed on the foundation row there is no need to work on a larger hook.

Make an even number of chains.

Foundation row 1 tr (dc) in 4th ch from hook *2 tr (dc) in next ch, miss 1 ch, rep from * to last ch, 1 tr (dc) in last ch, 3 ch, turn.

Patt row *2 tr (dc) in sp between the 2 tr (dc) stems worked in same ch of foundation row. Rep from * to last st, 1 tr (dc) in last st, 3 ch, turn.

Rep patt row for desired length (*figure 5c*).

CROSSED TREBLES (DOUBLE CROCHET)

The one problem that occasionally arises with this pattern is that there are more stitches at the end of the row than at the beginning. This occurs because it is not always obvious which stitches have been crocheted into and sometimes a stitch is accidentally worked into twice. This can be avoided if the stitches are counted on each row until the pattern becomes familiar. Note also that the hook is always inserted from front to back even though the stitches are crossing.

Make an even number of chains.

Foundation row 1 tr (dc) in 4th ch from hook *miss 1 ch, 1 tr (dc) in next ch, 1 tr (dc) in ch just missed. Rep from * to last ch, 1 tr (dc) in last ch, 3 ch, turn.

Patt row *Miss 1 tr (dc), 1 tr (dc) in next st, 1 tr (dc) in st just missed, rep from * to last st, 1 tr (dc) in last st, 3 ch, turn (*figure 5d*). This pattern looks even better if worked on alternate rows with a double crochet (single crochet) row between. This way the crossed trebles (double crochet) all go in the same direction.

CROCHET NETTING

This open fabric can be used as a base for surface crochet as well as being a fabric in its own right.

Chapter II shows how a netting effect of diamonds can be achieved using chains and slip stitch. Trebles (double crochet) and chain also give a netting effect, but this time of squares.

Make an odd number of chain.

Foundation row Work 1 tr (dc) in 6th ch from hook. (This includes the 3 turning ch plus the 1 ch for the 1st sp.) *1 ch, miss 1 st, 1 tr (dc) in next st, rep from * to end, 4 ch to turn.

Patt row *1 tr (dc) in next tr (dc), 1 ch, rep from * to last st, 1 tr (dc) in last st, 4 ch to turn. Repeat this row for the required length (*figure 5e*).

SECTION C

BED JACKET (*figure 6*)

The following bed jacket is in one piece being worked from one cuff edge across the body to the other. It will look like an oversized sweater without a head when it is completed.

To wear the bed jacket turn back approximately 10cm (4in) of the base of the 'sweater'. Place the arms in the sleeve cuffs and adjust to the figure in the manner of a stole.

Materials
4 balls Robin Aurora 4-ply
4.5mm (G) and 7.00mm (K) hooks

Measurement
To fit bust sizes 81-97cm (32-38in)

Tension
On 7.00mm (K) hook 9 sts to 10 cm (4in); 4 rows to 7cm (2¾in)

To make
With 7.00mm (K) hook work 27 ch.
Row 1 1 tr (dc) in 4th ch from hook *1 tr (dc) in next ch, rep from
* to end, 3 ch, turn.
Row 2 1 tr (dc) in same place as turning ch, (to inc 1), tr (dc) to last
st, 2 tr (dc) in last st, 3 ch, turn.
Row 3 2 tr (dc) in same place as turning ch, (to inc 2), tr (dc) to last
st, 3 tr (dc) in last st, 3 ch, turn.
Rep the last 2 rows until there are 55 sts. Make 23 ch on last row
plus a ch of 21 sts at beginning of row giving an extra 21 tr (dc) at
each end.
Work 44 rows without inc on these 97 sts.
Next row Dec 2 sts over next 3 sts, tr (dc) to last 3 sts, dec 2 sts over
last 3 sts, 3 ch, turn.
Next row Dec 1 st over next 2 sts, tr (dc) to last 2 sts, dec 1 st over
next 2 sts, 3 ch, turn.
Rep last 2 rows until 25 sts rem.

Cuffs
With 4.50mm (G) hook *put 2 tr (dc) in next 2 sts, 1 tr (dc) in next
st, rep from * to end. Work 5cm (2in) tr (dc).
Final row No turning chain, *miss 2 sts, 7 tr (dc) in next st, miss 2
sts, 1 dc (sc) in next st, rep from * to end.
Break off yarn. Work other cuff to match.
   Join seams by invisibly sewing them together as the seam may
show if carelessly joined.

Shell edge for main piece
Connect yarn to a seam with rs of work facing. *Work 7 tr (dc) in
top of next st, 1 dc (sc) in top of next st, rep from * to end.
   Fasten off.

DRESSING GOWN (*figure 7*).

Materials
40g balls of DK (worsted) in Light (L) 6 [7;7]; Medium (M) 10
[11;12]; Dark (D) 11 [12;13]
This was worked in Argyll 20 DK (worsted)
5.00mm (H) and 7.00mm (K) hooks.

Measurement
To fit bust sizes 76-81 [86-91;97-102] cm (30-32 [34-36;38-40]in)
Back length 140cm (55in)
Sleeve length (underarm) 41cm (16in)

Figure 6   *Bed jacket in trebles*
(double crochet)

Figure 7   *Dressing gown in 'V' sts
with curlicue ties at waist and on
hood, and with a needle-woven yoke*

33

Tension (gauge)
3 'V' sts to 5cm (2in), 10 rows to 12 cm (4¾in)

Fronts and back together
Work commences just below the bust with 5.00mm (H) 97 [109; 121] ch, in L.

Foundation row 2 tr (dc) in 5th ch from hook, *miss 1 ch, 2 tr (dc) in next ch, rep from * to last 2 ch, 1 tr (dc) in last ch, 3 ch, turn.

Patt row *2 tr (dc) in centre of 2 tr (dc) gr, rep from * to last st, 1 tr (dc) in last st, 3 ch, turn (46 [52; 58] 'V' sts plus 2 single sts at ends).

Work a further 8 rows patt.

Increase row for skirt *2 tr (dc) in centre of 'V' st, 2 tr (dc) in sp between 'V' sts, rep from * to last 3 sts, 2 tr (dc) in centre of 'V' st, 1 tr (dc) in last st, 3 ch, turn.

Work a further 14 rows in patt (approx length from foundation ch 30cm [12in]).

Change to M and work 30 rows in patt (approx length from foundation ch 66cm [26in]).

Change to D and work 35 rows in patt (approx length from foundation ch 106cm [42in]).

Break off yarn.

Turn work upside down and crochet again into foundation ch.

Bodice
Join in M, 3 ch, *2 tr (dc) in same place as gr on foundation row, rep from * to last st, 1 tr (dc) in last st, 3 ch, turn.

Work patt row 3 times.

Divide for front *2 tr (dc) in centre of 'V' st, rep from * 10 [12; 14] times, 1 tr (dc) in next tr, 3 ch, turn.

3 rows in patt in M.

Change to D. Work 10 rows in patt.

Break off yarn.

Divide for back Join M to rem tr (dc) on 'V' st where work divided for the front. 3 ch, *2 tr (dc) in centre of 'V' st, rep from * 21 [23; 25] times, 1 tr (dc) in next tr (dc), 3 ch, turn.

Rep patt row 3 times in M.

Work a further 10 rows patt in D.

Break off yarn.

Last front On remaining 24 [28; 32] sts work as for first front.

Sleeves (all sizes the same − 2 alike)
Make 55 ch in L on 5.00mm (H) hook. Work foundation row as for main piece (25 'V' sts). Work a further 22 patt rows. Break off L.

Join in M and work 5 patt rows. Break off M.

Join in D and work 7 patt rows in D.

1 row in cr st.

Break off yarn.

Hood
In L make 81 ch on 5.00mm (H) hook.

Work foundation row as for main piece (38 'V' sts).

Work 3 patt rows in L. Break off L.

Join in D and work 8 patt rows in D.

Break off yarn.

To join

Join shoulder seams by connecting the end 14 sts of back to the end 14 sts of corresponding front — the rest will be joined to the hood. Dc (sc) sleeves tog and insert into armholes. Attach hood to rem front and back neck sts.

Borders

Using D work 1 row dc (sc) up right front, round hood and down left front.
Work a second row dc (sc) up left front. *1 dc (sc), 1 ch, miss 1 st, rep from * to end of hood, dc (sc) down right front but include 5 buttonholes evenly spaced along bodice section (see p. 90), dc (sc) to hem, break off yarn.
Rejoin yarn to hem of left front and cr st round border.

Waist tie

With 7.00mm (K) hook and 6 strands of L yarn make a chain 150cm (59in) long. Thread this through the row of patt sts worked just before the inc row of the skirt.

Hood tie

With 5.00mm (H) hook and 3 strands of yarn work a length of ch 120cm (47in) long. Thread this through the holes in the dc (sc) border.

Curlicue (Make 4 in each colour.)

To make

10 ch, 5 tr (dc) in 3rd ch from hook *5 tr (dc) in next ch, rep from * to end. Break off yarn.
Attach one curlicue of each colour to each end of the ties at waist and neck.

EVENING TOP — BOOB TUBE (*figure 8*)

Materials

3 x 50g balls MS Sirdar Candlelight (worsted glitter)
1 x 50g ball C Sirdar Candlelight (worsted glitter)
4.00m (F) hook.

Measurement

To fit bust sizes 81-86 [91-97] cm (32-34 [36-38] in)
The finished article should measure 5-7cm (2-3in) less than the bust measurement as it stretches round the body.

Tension (gauge)

11 sts to 6cm ($2\frac{3}{8}$ in)

To make

With MS and 4.00mm (F) hook make 135 ch.
Row 1 work 1 tr (dc) in 4th ch from hook, 1 tr (dc) in each ch to end, 3 ch, turn.
Row 2 tr (dc) to end, 3 ch, turn.
Row 3 *miss 2 sts, 5 tr (dc) in next st, miss 2 sts, 1 tr (dc), rep from * 21 [24] times, 3 ch, turn.

Figure 8 Evening or summer top in a glitter yarn

Row 4 5 ch *work 5 tr (dc) leaving last lp of each st on hook, (as when decreasing, see p. 30), yoh, draw through all 6 lps — one 5trcl (5dccl) made. 2 ch, 1 tr (dc), 2 ch, rep from * to end, add 1 ch to 2 just made, for turning.
Row 5 & 6 as row 2.
Row 7 (ws will be facing) in C *1 ss (sl st), 1 tr (dc), rep from * to last st, 1 ss (sl st).
Row 8 as row 2.
Rep rows 2-8 incl 3 times and rows 2-7 once.
Join seam for centre front at the contrast points only.

Straps (4 in MS, 2 in C)
75 ch, cr st along this length.
Plait 2 MS and 1 C tog to form 1 strap and sew in position.

SECTION D

VARIATIONS FOR BED JACKET
a Use a contrasting yarn or a contrasting colour for the shell edge borders.
b Fold back lapels and attach wide ribbons at some point between throat and bust points, as ties.
c Use it for an evening jacket in a 4-ply glitter yarn.
d An alternative type of evening jacket can be made by using a smooth 4-ply yarn and threading narrow satin or velvet ribbon at regular intervals through the treble (double crochet) stitches.
e Work the pattern without increasing or decreasing to make a narrower stole-type bed jacket.

VARIATIONS FOR DRESSING GOWN
a Omit the hood and attach two squares for patch pockets.
b This pattern makes an excellent spring/summer coat if made shorter.
c It also makes a glamorous evening coat if a textured (worsted) double knit yarn is used such as a brushed wool, acrylic bouclé, mohair or lurex. Two shades of grey and black, light, medium and dark navy, two soft tones with a darker shade of brown, etc. give an air of elegance.
d Substitute the border (when competent) with the one suggested on p. 58, working each layer in a different shade.
e Thread three strands of Medium through the Dark stripe of bodice and three strands of Dark through Medium stripe of bodice (*figure 7*).

VARIATIONS FOR EVENING TOP — BOOB TUBE
a Substitute the thin straps for broader ones made of one width of the diamond pattern.
b Make in one colour and an untextured yarn then line with a thin fabric of strong contrasting colour.
c Substitute the contrasting slip stitch and treble (double crochet) row with just trebles (double crochet). This makes the top a little deeper but allows narrow ribbon to be threaded through this row.
d Make small diamond pieces of the contrasting yarn to fit into the diamond shaped gaps of the centre front.

e Convert the top to an evening dress by working the top in two straight pieces to reach from the top of the bust line to the floor. Make two side panels of treble (double crochet) in a triangular shape for movement and fullness for a skirt.

CHOOSING A DESIGN

The following are guidelines to help you co-ordinate colour, style, type of stitch and type of yarn when creating a design.

a If the yarn is textured the stitch pattern should be simple, and the more textured the yarn the simpler the stitches.

b Soft bulky yarns such as baby quick knits, acrylic, 2- 3- and 4-plys etc. cannot hold their shape if there is a weighty yarn and/or heavy pattern being used for the borders.

c Plain yarns, particularly the aran types, show the stitch construction clearly, and these firm, smooth yarns are ideal to show off complex stitch patterns.

d The hook choice is important. For cobweb effects exceptionally large hooks can be used. Conversely, small hooks can be used to produce stiff, almost cardboard-like effects.

e The shape of the garment and the stitch pattern should complement each other. For example, if you choose a square sleeve and square neckline, a square angular stitch pattern will appeal to the eye. Similarly, shell edges go well on curved shapes or with curved stitch patterns.

f Should the design be chosen to go with a particular outfit, look at the way the outfit is woven, or the shape of it, and try to carry some part of it into the crochet, e.g. a colour, a stitch shape or pattern shape.

g Remember a good contrasting or complementary colour is always better than a bad match.

h The figure type is important too. Stripes give optical illusions:
  i Horizontal stripes widen the figure.
  ii Vertical stripes narrow the figure.
  iii If grading the tones in one colour, with the lighter shades in the centre and the darker shades at the side, the figure will seem thinner. The opposite is true if the colours are reversed.
  iv Height can be given by having the darker shades near the shoulder and the hem, with the light tones at the waist (as with the dressing gown).
  v Yokes or raglan sleeves flatter narrow or sloping shoulders.
  vi Small, rotund people should avoid belts and waistbands and try to create an illusion of height.

i Remember the function of the design. It is no good having loopy, lacy effects in the fabric for a utility garment — the loops would just catch. Similarly, a close textured garment does not allow the feeling of femininity for an evening function.

V Textured Trebles

SECTION A

A treble (double crochet) is a very suitable stitch for introducing texture into a fabric. By inserting the hook around the stem of a treble (double crochet) the stitch then made is either lifted forwards or pushed backwards. Bobbles create texture also, giving a lumpy embossed look to a fabric. These are made either by putting groups of stitches in the same place, or using taller stitches in a short stitch row (see Chapter VI).

Crochet can achieve, in two ways, fabrics similar to those of the knitted fisherman's gansey or aran sweater, either by incorporating the textured effect whilst working the fabric or by adding a textured effect afterwards. This kind of crochet has a tendency to use more yarn.

RAISED TREBLES (DOUBLE CROCHET) (Rtr [Rdc]): 2 chain to turn.

Forward raised treble (double crochet) (RtrF [RdcF])
To make a Rtr (Rdc) that will stand forward from its neighbouring sts, yoh and insert the hook from right to left round the stem of the st below instead of through the top of the st in the normal way (*figure 9*). Yoh and draw the hook from behind the stem (3 lps are now on the hook). *Yoh, draw through 1st 2 lps. Repeat from * once. A raised treble (double crochet) at the front of the work has been made.

Backward raised treble (double crochet) (RtrB [RdcB])
A Rtr (Rdc) pushed to the back can be made in a similar way, but by inserting the hook round the stem of the tr (dc) from back to front and right to left. Thus, the stem of the st has been picked up from behind, so pulling the st to the back of the work (*figures 10 and 11*).

This type of stitch shows up clearly when worked in lines one on top of the other. Work one row of raised trebles (double crochet) at the front, and the next row of raised trebles (double crochet) at the back, to give smooth vertical rows on one side of the fabric and chain stitch horizontal rows on the other, thus a treble (double crochet) is worked round the stem of a stitch instead of inserting the hook into the top of the stitch in the usual manner. This leaves the top of the stitch free. It is well to watch for this point, and should there be more stitches at the end of the row than there ought to be, look behind the raised trebles (double crochet) to see if the stitch top has been accidentally used.

CLUSTERS (cl) : 3 chain to turn.
One of the difficulties with crochet is the lack of standardization of stitch names. The term cluster is given to many stitch patterns where stitches are drawn together at the top, sometimes the stitches are worked in the same place and sometimes the stitches are worked into consecutive stitch tops. The one described here has all the stitches placed in the same place.

Figure 9 Raised treble (double crochet) to the right. Safety pin shows stitch top not being worked into, as the hook picks up the treble (double crochet) stem of row below

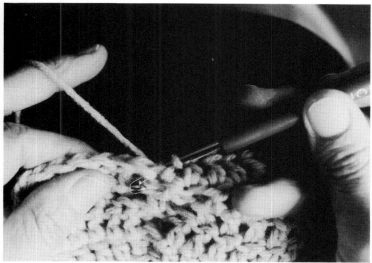

Figure 10 Hook is inserted from back to front when making a raised treble (double crochet) back

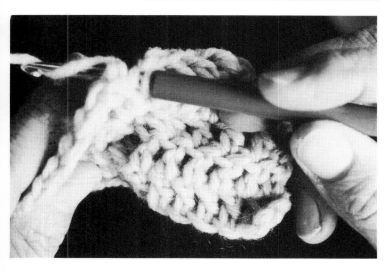

Figure 11 The hook is then taken to the back of the work round the treble (double crochet) stem before collecting yarn to complete the stitch

Three treble (double crochet) cluster (3trcl [3dccl])

Work a tr (dc) until 2 lps are left on the hook; work another tr (dc) in the same place until 3 lps are left on the hook; work a 3rd tr (dc) still in the same st until 4 lps are left on the hook, yoh, and draw through all 4 lps. One three treble (double crochet) cluster made (*figure 12a*).

Four treble (double crochet) cluster (4trcl [4dccl])

This is worked as above but a 4th tr (dc) is put in the same st and worked until 5 lps loops remain on the hook. The yarn is then drawn through the 5 lps remaining on the hook.

Once clusters have been introduced into a fabric there is a right and wrong side to the work. For the best effect include the clusters in the rows that are being worked with the wrong side of the fabric facing the crocheter. Tighter, more pronounced bobbles can be created by making four treble (double crochet) clusters in a double crochet (single crochet) row or by using a slip stitch instead of a double crochet (single crochet) (*figure 12b*).

The following pattern idea incorporates both raised trebles (double crochet) and clusters. Using aran wool and a 5.00mm (H) hook to get a crisp textured finish, make 17 ch.

Row 1 1 tr (dc) in 4th ch from hook, 1 tr (dc) in each st to the end, 3 ch, turn.

Row 2 *1 RtrB (RdcB), 1 tr (dc), 1 4trcl (4dccl), 1 tr (dc), rep from * twice, 1 RtrB (RdcB), 1 tr (dc), 3 ch, turn.

Row 3 *1 RtrF (RdcF), 3 tr (dc), rep from * twice, 1 RtrF (RdcF), 1 tr (dc), 3 ch, turn.

Rep rows 2 and 3 until required length is reached.

To make this pattern wider increase the number of stitches by a multiple of four.

SECTION B

By using only trebles (double crochet) and chains in the various ways described both above and in Chapter IV, dozens of crochet fabrics can be made. There is not sufficient space in these pages to give in detail more than a few, but this is an advantage as you can find out for yourself what happens when the hook is inserted at different angles and when stitches are increased and then decreased in the same row.

*Figure 12   a three treble cluster (double crochet cluster) worked in trebles (double crochet) **b** four treble cluster (treble cluster) worked in double crochets (single crochets), **c** popcorns worked between columns of raised trebles (double crochet), **d** raised trebles (double crochet) rib — one stitch to the front, one stitch to the back, **e** raised treble (double crochet) rib using two stitches to the front two sts to the back, **f** as **e** but instead of working the pairs of stitches to form columns of ridges, they are worked alternately to give a basket weave*

a   b   c

POPCORN STITCH (P)

Clusters can flatten with use, particularly in soft acrylics and wool yarns, but the popcorn stitch retains its texture even after pressing. Pressing crochet is *not* recommended however except for firm cottons.

   With rs of the crochet facing, work 6 tr (dc) into the same st. Remove the hook from the st and insert it from front to back into the top of the 1st of the 6 tr (dc) made (*figure 12c*). Collect the loose lp from the last of the 6 tr (dc) and draw it through to the front. Continue crocheting along the row in the normal way.

   Popcorn stitches require at least two other plain stitches between them if they are not to look squashed and untidy. This is one of the few textured stitches worked with the right side of the fabric facing.

RAISED TREBLE (DOUBLE CROCHET) RIB

An elasticated welt or band can be made by working rows of: *1 RtrF (RdcF), 1 RtrB (RdcB), rep from * to end . The thing always to remember is to work the ridge that pokes forwards as a RtrF (RdcF) and the ridge that sinks backwards as a RtrB (RdcB). The greater the number of rows made, the more elastic the 'rib' becomes. It also helps to use smaller hook sizes if this pattern is to be used at cuffs, neck and waist. One further point: a Rtr (Rdc) rib is most rigid, i.e. least elastic, when it is started at the foundation chain. Therefore *make sure* that the last row of the rib is the end of the work (*figure 12d*).

SECTION C

RAGLAN SWEATER (*figure 13*)

9 [9; 10] Lopi 100g hanks
5.00mm (H) and 7.00mm (K) hooks.

Measurement
To fit bust/chest sizes 81-89 [92-99; 102-112] cm (32-35 [36-39; 40-44] in)
Underarm sleeve length 45cm (17¾in)
Back length 66cm (26in)

d   e   f

Figure 13 *His and her raglan sweater in thick yarn*

Tension (gauge)

8 trs (dcs) to 7cm (2¾in) 4 rows to 7cm (2¾in)
Work is from the neck to waist and neck to cuff edges. Chains must be worked loosely or the neck band will fit badly.

Front

Size 81-89cm (32-35in) only
Row 1 Using 7.00mm (K) make 4 ch, 2 tr (dc) in 1st ch of 4 ch made, 3 ch, turn.
Row 2 Work in tr (dc) and inc 1 st at each end, 3 ch, turn.
Row 2a Tr (dc) to end ** 11 ch, break off yarn.
Make another piece up to **, 3 ch, turn.
Continue as for all sizes.

Sizes 92-99 [102-112] cm (36-39) [40-44] in)
Row 1 Using 7.00mm (K) hook make 4 ch, 3 tr (dc) in 1st ch of 4 ch made, 3 ch, turn.
Row 2 Work in tr (dc) and inc 1 st each end** 11 ch, break off yarn.
Make another triangle up to **, 3 ch, turn.

All sizes
Row 3 1 tr (dc) in same place as turning ch, 4 tr (dc), 11 tr (dc), across chain of 1st piece, 4 tr (dc) across 2nd triangle, 2 tr (dc) in last st, (23 sts), 3 ch, turn.
Row 4 1 tr (dc) in same place as turning ch, 2 tr (dc), 1P, *7 tr (dc), 1P, rep from * once, 2 tr (dc), 2 tr (dc) in next st. Work 3 rows tr (dc) inceasing 1 st at each end.

Size 81-89cm (32-35in) only
Rep last 4 rows once. Work Row 4 once. Work 2 rows tr (dc) inc 1 st at each end, (47 sts).

Size 92-99cm (36-39in) only
Rep last 4 rows twice.
Work Row 4 once.
Work 1 row tr (dc) inc 1 st at each end, (53 sts).

Size 102-112cm (40-44in) only
Rep last 4 rows, 3 times.
Work Row 4 once.
Work 1 row tr (dc) inc 1 st at each end, (61 sts).

All sizes
Work 1 row RtrF (RdcF) inc 1 st at each end. This gives a ridge on the rs.
Work 12 [14; 16] rows tr (dc).
Change to 5.00mm (H) hook, work 6 rows Rtr (Rdc) rib (see p. 41).

Back
With 7.00mm (K) hook make 21 ch.
Row 1 2 tr (dc) in 4th ch from hook, 14 tr (dc), 2 tr (dc) in last ch, 3 ch, turn.
Row 2 1 tr (dc) in same place as turning ch, tr (dc) to last st, 2 tr (dc) in last ch, 3 ch, turn.

Row 2a (size 81-89cm [32-35in] only) tr (dc) to end, 3 ch, turn.
Row 3 As row 2.
Work as Front from row 4.

Sleeves (2 alike)
With 7.00mm (K) hook make 11 ch.
Row 1 2 tr (dc) in 4th ch from hook, 6 tr (dc), 2 tr (dc) in last ch, 3 ch, turn.
Row 2 1 tr (dc) in same as turning ch, tr (dc) to last st, 2 tr (dc) in last st.
Row 2a (size 81-89cm [32-35in] only) tr (dc) to end, 3 ch, turn.
Row 3 As row 2.
Work as front from row 4 to end of yoke. i.e., finishing with RtrF (RdcF) row.
Work 1 row tr (dc) without incs.
Next row Dec 1 st over 2, tr (dc) to last 2 sts, dec 1 st over 2, 3 ch, turn (see p. 40).
Work 3 rows tr (dc).
Rep the last 4 rows, 4 times.
Work 1 further row dec.
Work 2 rows tr (dc).
Change to 5.00mm (H) hook work 6 rows Rtr (Rdc) rib.
Join yoke seams together on the rs with cr st using 7.00mm (K) hook.
With 5.00mm (H) hook work 6 rows Rtr (Rdc) rib round neck using 48 [50; 54] sts.
Join sleeve and underarm seams.

ARAN SWEATER AND DRESS (*figure 14*)
There are many different ways to write crochet patterns. The format set out here is different from the others as it gives you the complete 6-row pattern and leaves the crocheter to make sure that there is a continuity of pattern. In this instance the diamonds follow on.

Materials
8 [9] x Aran 50g balls

Measurement
To fit sizes 84-92 [97-102] cm (33-36 [38-40] in)

Tension (gauge)
9 tr (dc) to 7cm (2¾in) on 5.00mm (H) hook (you may need 5.50mm (I) hook) 4 rows to 5cm (2in).

Additional abbreviations
RtrFL (RdcFL) - left   RtrFR (RdcFR) - right
RtrBL (RdcBL) - left   RtrBR (RdcBR) - right
These are rows of trebles (double crochet) worked round the raised trebles (double crochet) of the previous row to bring them across from left to right and from right to left (*figure 15*).
The L indicates the stitch leans to the left, the R indicates the stitch leans to the right.
The pattern is worked into 1 row tr (dc) using only 17 sts. The rest of the stitches are tr (dc).
Row 1 2 RtrF (RdcF), 1 tr (dc), 1 RtrFR (RdcFR), 5 tr (dc),

Figure 14 Sweater and sweater dress incorporating embroidery into the diamond ridges

43

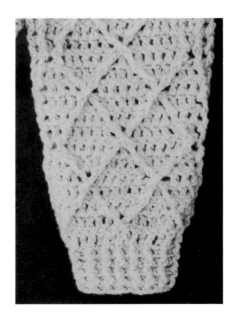

Figure 15 *Close up of raised trebles (double crochet) forming the diamond formation of the aran sweaters*

1 RtrFL (RdcFL), 1 ch, 1 RtrFR (RdcFR), 5 tr (dc), 1 RtrFL (RdcFL), 1 tr (dc), 2 RtrF (RdcF).
Row 2 2 RtrB (RdcB), 2 tr (dc), 1 RtrBL (RdcBL), 3 tr (dc), 1 RtrBR (RdcBR), 3 tr (dc), 1 RtrBL (RdcBL), 2 tr (dc), 2 RtrB (RdcB).
Row 3 2 RtrF (RdcF), 3 tr (dc), 1 RtrFL (RdcFL), 1 tr (dc), 1 RtrFR (RdcFR), 5 tr (dc), 1 RtrFL (RdcFL), 1 tr (dc), 1 RtrFR (RdcFR), 3 tr (dc), 2 RtrF (RdcF).
Row 4 2 RtrB (RdcB), 3 tr (dc), 1 RtrBR (RdcBR), 1 ch, 1 RtrBL (RdcBL) (to form a crossing of raised tr [dc]), 5 tr (dc), 1 RtrBR (RdcBR), 1 ch, 1 RtrBL (RdcBL), 3 tr (dc), 2 RtrB (RdcB).
Row 5 2 RtrF (RdcF), 2 tr (dc), 1 RtrFR (RdcFR), 3 tr (dc), 1 RtrFL (RdcFL), 3 tr (dc), 1 RtrFR (RdcFR), 3 tr (dc), 1 RtrFL (RdcFL), 2 tr (dc), 2 RtrF (RdcF).
Row 6 2 RtrB (RdcB), 1 tr (dc), 1 RtrBR (RdcBR), 5 tr (dc), 1 RtrBL (RdcBL), 1 tr (dc), 1 RtrBR (RdcBR), 5 tr (dc), 1 RtrBL (RdcBL), 1 tr (dc), 2 RtrB (RdcB).
NB: On the last repeat of row 6, tr (dc) the last tr (dc) and Rtr (Rdc) as though making a cl but work as 2 separate sts on Row 1, this helps to give the end diamond a point.
The raised trebles (double crochet) in this pattern need to be looped up and lifted a little to make the stitches longer to lie flat along the work.

Body back
Make 56 [65] ch.
Work 1 tr (dc) in 4th ch from hook, tr (dc) to end, 3 ch, turn, (54 [63] sts).
Work 23 [25] rows tr (dc).
Next row Ss (sl st) over 2 [6] sts, tr (dc) to last 2 [6] sts, 3 ch, turn
Work 24 rows in tr (dc) on these 50 [51] sts. Break off yarn.

Front
Make 56 [65] ch.
Work 1 row tr (dc).
Next row (rs) 35 [40] tr (dc) (including turning ch), Patt row 1 over 17 sts, tr (dc) 2 [6] sts, 3 ch, turn.
Keep continuity of the patt panel and keep the rest of the front plain tr (dc), work 22 [24] rows.
Next row Ss (sl st) over 2 [6] patt 17, tr (dc) to last 2 [6] sts, 3 ch, turn.
Work 18 rows. Break off yarn.

Sleeves (2 alike)
Make 33 ch.
1 tr (dc) in 4th ch from hook, tr (dc) to end, 3 ch, turn.
Next row 1 tr (dc) in same place as turning ch, 4 tr (dc) patt 17, 4 tr (dc) 2 tr (dc) in last st.
Keeping patt continuity, inc 1 st at each end of every 3rd row until work measures 42.5cm (16¾in).
Work 19 rows on centre 19 sts in patt. This leaves 2 single tr (dc) for joining.
Work 6cm (2⅜in) of Rtr (Rdc) rib at cuffs using 4.00mm (F) hook and working into original foundation row of sleeve. Join seams.

Welt

Work 6cm ($2^3/_8$ in) of Rtr (Rdc) rib using foundation ch of front and back and 4.00mm (F) hook (see p. 41).

SECTION D

VARIATIONS FOR RAGLAN SWEATER
a Crochet the bobbles in a contrasting colour.
b Have popcorns in only the front yoke and attach 'clappers' to imitate bells (*figure 13*).
c Crochet the whole of the yoke in a deeper shade.
d Make the neck a polo neck.
e Use the basic style as a flat raglan without incorporating either the raised tr (dc) row or the popcorns.

VARIATIONS FOR THE ARAN DESIGN
a Have the pattern on one sleeve only.
b Embroider flowers in the centre of the diamonds (*figure 14*).
c Continue the raised treble (double crochet) rib by another 9-14cm (3½-5½in) for a polo neck.
d Put a contrasting coloured yarn in cr st as a surface crochet on top of the raised sts.
e Work more front and back rows before sleeve shapings, to make a shift dress.

TEXTURED WAISTCOAT
Taking the steps in design one stage further I have included the following half written pattern which is a short waistcoat/bolero top illustrated in colour plate 3 and is designed to allow you to experiment with texture and colour. It is a basic shape that fits the figure primarily because of the choice of stitch for the waistband and also because the double crochet (single crochet) bands are subtly shaped. The main body of the work consists of two pieces of unshaped, textured crochet. The principles behind the design are simple:
a It is a basic rectangular shape, which allows the imagination free-reign without having to cope with increases and decreases.
b Where a textured stitch is introduced it is worked in a textured yarn thus doubling the 'crunchy', 'bobbly', 'hairy' properties of the yarns.
c The main pieces which are in stripes, have the stripes worked from side to centre back, giving an optically narrowing and lengthening effect to the figure (*figure 16*).
d The final borders are the means used for a good fit.
As this is not a crochet pattern in the accepted sense, you may find the points given below helpful.
a the length can be adjusted by adding pairs of stitches or removing pairs of stitches.
b the fabric is not made using any one spinner's range of yarn, but by mixing many makes — British, American and imported. Discontinued lines or the oddments box ease the cost.
c Remember all textured stitches are worked on the wrong side and to avoid bias it is therefore advisable to work the rows in between on the right side.

Figure 16 *Textured waistcoat – a do-it-yourself design*

d The whole is worked in DDK (Afghan) but two DK (worsted) yarns can be worked together or alternatively three strands of 3-ply can be used to give the DDK thickness. This adds to the possible colour combinations, shading etc. within the garment.

e Each row of the main pieces can be worked in different yarns and it is not necessary to make the two pieces symmetrical. However, if this is your first adventure in colour crochet and texture it is suggested that you make both pieces alike, working one row on one piece and then the same row on the other piece.

f Choose the colour for the borders and waistband carefully, as this is the major contribution to the overall aesthetic appearance of the waistcoat, holding the oddments together as a complete whole.

g If the garment is being made for a fuller figure aim to have the lightest shades in the centre back and centre front, grading to the darkest shades under the arms, this combined with the downward stripes will be more flattering.

h Again for the fuller figure do not make a waistband, and have a longer line.

i The garment launders well in a cold water wash, and there are special detergents on the market to make this possible.

To make

Use a 7.00mm (K) hook for size 87-92 (34-36in). Use a 9.00mm (wood 15) hook for the 2 main pieces in sizes 97-102cm (38-40in) and a 7.00mm (k) hook for borders and waistband.

Yarn should be thickness of DDK (Afghan) throughout the body piece.

Make 77 ch in a smooth yarn.

Row 1 1 tr (dc) in 4th ch from hook, tr (dc) to end, (75 sts). Break off yarn.

Row 2 With ws facing join in a mohair yarn, *3trcl (3dccl), 1 ss (sl st), rep from * to end. Break off yarn.

Row 3 With a smooth yarn and ws facing. Work in htr (hdc).

Row 4 In the same yarn and rs facing work in tr (dc). Break off yarn.

Row 5 With ws facing join in bouclé yarn, *1 RtrB (RdcB), 1 dc (sc), rep from * to end. Break off yarn.

Row 6 With rs facing and a smooth yarn work in tr (dc). Break off yarn. This can be a harsh colour.

Row 7 With ws facing join in a semi-textured colour yarn *1 tr (dc) anchored into top of Rtr (Rdc) on row 5 and looping the yarn up so that it does not pull, 1 dc (sc) rep from * to end. Break off yarn.

Row 8 With rs facing and smooth yarn tr (dc) to end. Break off yarn.

Row 9 With ws facing join in mohair yarn *1 tr(dc), 1 ss (sl st), rep from * to end. Break off yarn.

Row 10 With rs facing and smooth yarn, tr (dc) to end. Break off yarn.

Row 11 With rs facing join in a smooth multicoloured yarn * 1 RtrF (RdcF) worked round stem of tr (dc) of row below, 1 tr (dc), rep from * until 33 sts including the joining st, have been worked, (42 unworked sts). Break off yarn.

Row 12 With ws facing and on the 33 worked sts, join in a bouclé yarn *1 tr (dc), 1 ss (sl st), rep from * to end. Break off yarn.

Row 13 With rs facing and a smooth yarn tr (dc) to end. Break off yarn.
Row 14 With ws facing join in a chenille yarn *1 tr (dc), 1 ss (sl st) rep from * to end. Break off yarn.
Row 15 With rs facing and a smooth yarn work in tr (dc) to end. Break off yarn.

Right hand body piece
Work as lh until Row 10 is completed.
Work Rows 11-15 inclusive on the *last* 33 sts when rs is facing.
Join the 2 pieces together with cr st on the rs or alternatively stitch them together decoratively.

Side borders
In a smooth DDK (Afghan) yarn and 7.00mm (K) hook work 3 rows in dc (sc). Lose 1 st on every row at the shoulder point by working 2 sts together. Place ws of back and front tog and on the rs join the 2 pieces together with cr st for 15 sts. Do not break off yarn but continue round the armhole with cr st on the rs missing every 5th st for a good fit. Fasten off.

Waistband
For a 72cm (27in) waist — (add extra sts accordingly to vary the waist.)
Work 95 tr (dc) evenly into the crochet of the main piece at waist level using a smooth DDK (Afghan) yarn.
Next row 2 ch, *1 RtrF (RdcF), 1 RtrB (RdcB), rep from * to end. Rep this row until 7-9cm (3-4in) has been worked. Do not break off yarn.

Front border
Dc (sc) up front to shoulder point, dc (sc) across back neck using no more than 10 sts, dc (sc) down other front. Work a further 4 rows dc (sc) losing 1 st on each row at shoulder points and putting 3 button-holes in waistband, by missing 1 st and replacing it with a ch (see p. 90). With rs facing work 1 row cr st, missing every 6th st after the waistband. Fasten off. Stitch on buttons to correspond with button-holes.

VI Long Trebles

Diagram 15

Diagram 16

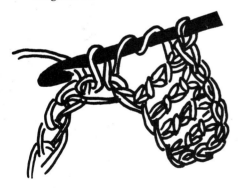

Diagram 17

SECTION A

Long trebles, as their name implies, are tall stitches and are made by wrapping the yarn more than once around the hook before inserting it into the work. These loops are removed in twos in the same manner as they are removed in a treble (double crochet). It is well to be reminded at this point that all crochet starts with a loop and no matter how complicated the working of the stitch, it will aways end with one loop on the hook, and this loop is not counted as a stitch.

Any height of stitch can be obtained by wrapping the yarn round the hook several times and removing the loops in twos.

DOUBLE TREBLE (TREBLE): (dtr [tr]): 4 chain to turn.

To make a dtr (tr) wrap the yarn round the hook twice, insert the hook into the work going under 2 strands as usual. Place yoh and draw to the front of the work. There are now 4 lps on the hook, *yoh, and draw through 2 lps. Repeat from * twice — one double treble (treble) made (*diagram 15*).

TRIPLE TREBLE (DOUBLE TREBLE): (tr tr [dtr]): 5 chain to turn.

To make a tr tr (dtr) wrap the yarn round the hook 3 times. Insert the hook as usual into work, yoh and draw the thread through to the front. This gives 5 lps on the hook *yoh and draw through 2 lps. Repeat from * 3 times — one triple treble (double treble) made (*diagram 16*).

QUADRUPLE TREBLE (TRIPLE TREBLE) (quad tr [tr tr]): 6 chain to turn.

To make a quad tr (tr tr) wrap the yarn round the hook 4 times. Insert the hook into the work, yoh and draw the thread through to the front. There are now 6 lps on the hook. *yoh and draw through 2 lps. Repeat from * 4 times — one quadruple treble (triple treble) made (*diagram 17*).

TO INCREASE

To inc by 1, in any st, is just a matter of putting 2 sts in one hole. This applies whether the inc is at the beginning, end or middle of a row.

To inc by a large number of sts in long tr work is described for trs (dc), (see p. 30).

TO DECREASE

To dec by 1 work the 1st st until 2 lps are left on the hook, then work the 2nd st until there are only 3 lps left on the hook, yoh and draw through these remaining 3 lps. This gives 1 ch top over 2 sts. It is not important how many lps the st began with — this simple rule applies to all basic sts with the exception of a htr (hdc) (see p. 57).

To decrease by a large number of sts follow the method described for trs (dc), (see p. 30).

Using aran wool and a 5.00mm (H) hook practise the different

Plate 4   *Long trebles are used to blend colours*

Plate 5   *Nature can often be a source of inspiration for patterns; the heather hills of Lancashire and a selection of 'Wendy' yarns prompted this design*

Plate 6   *Surface crochet using a random dyed bouclé,
worked into an open-weave fabric*

Plate 7   *The coat was designed from the
mittens. Large initial palm and gauntlet
motifs were made and joined together with
the design on the tips of the fingers of the
mittens. Matching ties and pockets copied
from the backs of the mittens were added last
of all*

long trebles and compare them with samples made previously in double crochet (single crochet) and treble (double crochet). It is advised that the samples worked have straight sides as well as including increasing and decreasing as described above. It will be noted that the taller the stitch, the wider the fabric becomes (*figure 17*).

SECTION B

There are certain disadvantages to using long trebles as a fabric by itself particularly when wrapping the yarn three or more times round the hook. These are:
a There is little substance to the fabric and so unless it is worked in fine cotton it has a tendency to lose its shape.
b The stitches easily catch on items like door handles etc.
c Sleeves of long trebles droop and can get in the way.
Its advantages are:-
a It grows very quickly and is most suitable for stoles, scarves, bed-jackets, etc.
b If one row of long trebles is worked occasionally in a fabric of another firmer pattern, it adds interest to the overall effect as a contrasting texture.
c It is ideal for using as a base stitch to allow ribbon, elastic, cords, etc. to be threaded through, either for a decorative effect, or for holding ties at the waist or throat.

BOUCLÉ STITCH (using a double treble [treble])
Another way of using long trebles is to put them in a row of shorter stitches to give a textured effect.

As mentioned previously there is no right or wrong side to crochet until it is made to have one. With the bouclé stitch the work has a smooth side and a textured side. The textured side is the 'right' side in this fabric. When crocheting the bouclé stitch, the wrong or smooth side of the work should be facing to allow the tall double trebles (trebles) to bend double to form a small loop between the short double crochet (single crochet) stitches. This means that it is only worked on every alternate row.

Make a length of ch which gives an odd number of sts. Work 1 row of either tr (dc) or dc (sc).
Patt row (ws facing)
1 ch to turn — *1 dtr (tr), 1 dc (sc) rep from * to end (*figure 18a*).

BOXES (using a quadruple treble (triple treble))
As shown in the previous chapter, trebles (double crochet) do not only need to be worked into the tops of other stitches or in the spaces made by chains etc., they can also be worked around the stem part to give a raised effect. The box pattern described here uses the height of the quadruple treble (triple treble) to break the monotony of a striped fabric worked in rows of trebles (double crochet) three rows below. The quadruple treble (triple treble) is thus lying flat over the top of the contrasting stripe in the fabric (*figure 18b*).

For a dramatic effect use two contrasting colours of the same type of yarn.

In the MS make a length of ch that can be divided by 4 with 1

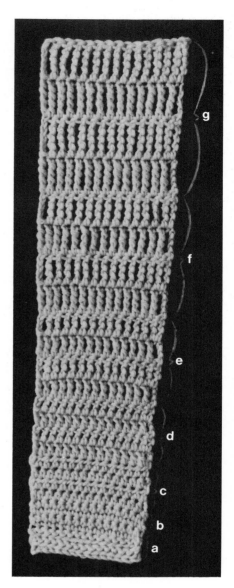

Figure 17 a slip stitch worked into one loop only to allow a little growth b double crochet (single crochet), c half treble (half double crochet), d treble (double crochet), e double treble (treble) f triple treble (double treble) g quadruple treble (triple treble) – note how the larger stitches spread

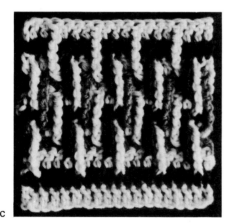

left over.

Foundation row 1 tr (dc) in 4th ch from hook, 1 tr (dc) in each ch to end, 3 ch, turn. (Sts should divide by 4 with 3 left over.)

Row 1 In MS tr (dc) to last st. Join in C in last st to avoid a colour drag, 3 ch, turn (see p. 14).

Row 2 In C tr (dc) to end, 3 ch, turn.

Row 3 In C tr (dc) to last st, join MS in at top of last st, 3 ch, turn.

Row 4 In MS 1 tr (dc), 1 quad tr (tr tr) round st of tr (dc) 3 rows below (i.e. last row of MS), 3 tr (dc), work from * to last 2 sts, 1 quad tr (tr tr) round st of tr (dc) 3 rows below, 1 tr (dc), 3 ch, turn.

NB: The quadruple treble (triple treble) is a stitch, so there should be one unworked chain top lying behind each quadruple treble (triple treble).

Rep rows 1-4 until the required length is reached.

To finish break off yarn after working row 1.

COLOUR SHADING WITH LONG TREBLES (using triple treble [double treble])

The box pattern described above contains a dropped long treble because of the way the quadruple treble (triple treble) is incorporated. The following pattern however uses dropped triple trebles (double trebles) throughout to create a woven effect. It also enables colours to be blended and softened (*colour plate 5*) unlike the box pattern which generally creates a dramatic contrast. This pattern requires concentration as it is all too easy to both gain and lose stitches. In addition, the dropped triple treble (double treble) when worked must be checked on each row to make sure that they have been anchored in the right place along the whole row. Again it is quite easy (particularly when working from the wrong side) to anchor the triple treble (double treble) at an angle. Use three colours of the same type of yarn. The colours should either all blend gently with each other or two colours to blend and one to contrast (*figure 18c*). Three separate colours that are totally uncomplementary give a dazzling effect that can be very harsh to the eyes.

With MS make a length of chain that can be divided by 3 leaving 3 ch over.

Row 1 1 tr (dc) in 4th ch from hook, tr (dc) to end. Join in 1st C, 3 ch, turn.

Row 2 Tr (dc) to end, join in MS, 3 ch, turn.

Row 3 Tr (dc) to end, join in 2nd C, 3 ch, turn.

Row 4 Tr (dc) to end, join in MS, 3 ch, turn.

Row 5 1 tr (dc), 1 tr tr (dtr) round stem at front of tr (dc) 2 rows below, *2 tr (dc), 1 tr tr (dtr) round stem at front of tr (dc) 2 rows below, rep from * to end, join in 1st C, 3 ch, turn.

Row 6 1 tr (dc), 1 tr tr (dtr) round stem at back of tr (dc) 2 rows below, * 2 tr (dc), 1 tr tr (dtr) round stem at back of tr (dc) 2 rows below, rep from * to end, join in MS, 3 ch, turn.

Row 7 *1 tr tr (dtr) round stem at front of tr (dc) 2 rows below, 2 tr (dc) rep from * to last 2 sts, 1 tr tr (dtr) round stem at front of tr (dc) 2 rows below, 1 tr (dc). Join in 2nd C, 3 ch, turn.

Row 8 Tr (dc) to end, join in MS, 3 ch, turn.

Rep rows 5-8 until fabric reaches the required length.

Experiment with this idea using four colours and quadruple trebles (triple trebles) or five colours and quintruple trebles (quadruple trebles) (i.e. wrapping the yarn round the hook five times).

Figure 18 Use of long trebles **a** double treble (treble) in a bouclé stitch **b** quadruple treble (triple treble) to form boxes, **c** triple treble (double treble) to shade colours

Figure 19 Stitches of different height worked round the stem of one stitch to form 'pockets'

Also experiment with long trebles by using the various heights to achieve patterns (*figure 19*). The row has *1 quad tr (tr tr), 1 tr tr (dtr), 1 dtr (tr), 1 tr (dc) all worked round the stem of 1 st with 1 dc (sc) worked into the top of the same st. This gives a chunky textured effect and can also give an interesting colour effect.

SECTION C

CLOAK (*colour plate 2*)
This is a simple pattern but it gives the wearer a feeling of floating.

Materials
7 balls Robin Harlequin Chunky Slub
8 balls Wendy Monaco Chunky brushed
12.00mm (Jumbo size wood 20) and 9.00mm (wood 15) hooks.
Sizes and Tension (gauge) are omitted as not being applicable.
Make two or more cloaks each in a different yarn. The illustration (*figure 20*) shows three layers.
With 12.00mm (Jumbo wood 20) hook make 38 ch.
Row 1 1 tr tr (dtr) in 6th ch from hook, *1 ch, 1 tr tr (dtr) in next ch, rep from * to end, 5 ch, turn.
Row 2 1 tr tr (dtr) in same place as turning ch, *1 ch, 2 tr tr (dtr) in next tr tr (dtr). Rep from * to end, 6 ch, turn.
Row 3 1 tr tr (dtr) on next tr tr (dtr), *1 ch, 1 tr tr (dtr) in next tr tr (dtr), rep from * to end, 6 ch, turn.
Row 4 1 tr tr (dtr) in next tr tr (dtr), *1 ch, 1 tr tr (dtr) in next ch, 2 ch, 1 tr tr (dtr) in next tr tr (dtr), rep from * to end, 6 ch, turn.
Row 5 1 tr tr (dtr) in next tr tr (dtr), 2 ch, 1 tr tr (dtr) in next tr tr (dtr), rep from * to end, 6 ch, turn.
Rep row 5 to required length.

To make up
Using the yarn of the top layer and 9.0mm (wood 15) hook, cr st the layers of cloak together at fronts leaving the hems loose.

Neck band
Dc (sc) the layers together with 9.00mm (wood 15) hook, and work 5cm (2in) in dc (sc) finishing with a cr st.

Figure 20 A cloak to feel and to wear, each layer moving on top of the other

Figure 21 The top is made of two shawls. The skirt is based on chevrons to give an illusion of pleats (for skirt pattern, see p. 000)

SHAWL TOP (*figure 21*)

Materials
16 balls Wendy Fashion 4-ply crepe
Matching shirring elastic
3.00 (C) and 4.00 (F) hooks.

Measurement
To fit bust size 87-92cm (34-36in). It will fit a larger or smaller bust as it is on elastic.

Tension (gauge)
7 sts to 5cm (2in) over dtr (tr)

To make (two pieces alike)
59 ch
Row 1 Work 3dtrcl (3trcl) 3 ch 3dtrcl (3trcl) 3 ch 3dtrcl (3trcl) all into 7th ch from hook, *miss 3 ch, 1 dtr (tr) in next ch, miss 3 ch, 3dtrcl (3trcl) 3 ch 3dtrcl (3trcl) 3 ch 3dtrcl (3trcl) in next ch, rep from * 5 times, miss 3 ch, 1 dtr (tr) in last ch, 4 ch, turn.
Row 2 1 dtr (tr) in sp before cl gr, *3 ch, 1 ss (sl st) in top of centre cl, 3 ch, 1 dtr (tr) in sp before dtr (tr) of row below, 1 dtr (tr) in sp after dtr (tr) of row below, rep from * to end working last dtr (tr) in top of turning ch, 4 ch, turn.
Row 3 1 dtr (tr) in sp before next st, 1 dtr (tr) in each dtr (tr) to next dtrcl (trcl), *1 dtrcl (trcl) 3 ch 1 dtrcl (trcl) 3 ch 1 dtrcl (trcl) in ss (sl st) of row below, 1 dtr (tr) in each st to next dtrcl (trcl) group, rep from * to end finishing with 1 dtr (tr) in top of turning ch, 4 ch, turn.

Rep the last 2 rows which gives an increase of 1 st between the columns of cls on every alternate row. The result is a triangular shawl without the point.

Continue until the work is long enough. Figure 21 shows the 1st variation of this patt and took 43 rows.

Border
Make a shell edge of *1 dtrcl (trcl) 3 ch 1 dtrcl (trcl) 3 ch 1 dtrcl (trcl) to form a group, miss 3 to 5 sts, 1 dc, miss 3 to 5 sts, rep from * to end. It is not possible to give an accurate border patt as it will alter if the length varies, but aim for 2 groups on the plain dtrs (trs) and 1 group on the cl group (*figure 22*).

Cuffs
With a 3.00mm (C) hook work 5cm (2in) raised tr (dc) rib (see p. 41).

To make up
a Place the shawl over the body and pin with a safety pin at the base point of the side seams. From this pin to the end of the cuff is the underarm seam.
b Dc (sc) the underarm sleeve seam tog on ws. At this stage there are 2 unconnected sleeves and 4 loose points.
c Place the 2 pieces back on the body and overlap the points to cross over the body as shown in the photograph. Pin these tog where they fit comfortably. Insert shirring elastic in the tops of the sts of

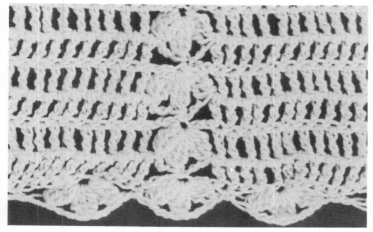

Figure 22 *Close up of the clusters used in the shawl top*

the final row before the shell edge was worked.

d Work 1 row tr (dc) round the waist connecting the 2 pieces tog.

e Make a 5cm (2in) raised tr (dc) rib as a waist band.

ZIPPERED JACKET (*figure 23*)

I cannot explain it but three people out of four work this pattern on a bias, although it has *no* bias. Please watch carefully that the very end dc (sc) is worked into with a tr (dc). The edges should be straight and vertical.

Measurements

To fit bust/chest sizes 81 [86; 92; 97; 102; 107; 112] cm (32 [34; 36; 38; 40; 42; 44] in)
Actual size: 84 [89; 95; 100; 105; 110; 115] cm (33 [35; 37½; 39½; 41½; 43¼; 45¼] in)
Back Length 54cm (21¼in)
Underarm sleeve length: 46cm (18in)

Materials

10 [12; 13; 14; 16; 17; 20] x 25g balls aran
5.00mm (H) hook.

Tension (gauge)

6 sts to 5cm (2in) 6 patt rows to 5.5cm (2¼in)

Main piece (front and back)

Make 108 [114; 120; 126; 132; 138; 144] ch
Row 1 1 dc (sc) in 3rd ch from hook, 1 dc (sc) in each ch to end,
3 ch, turn, (107 [113; 119; 125; 131; 137; 143] sts).
Row 2 *1 tr (dc) in back lp of next st, rep from * to end, 1 ch, turn.
Row 3 1 dc (sc) in each st to end, 3 ch, turn.
Rep Rows 2 and 3, 12 [12; 13; 13; 13; 14; 14] times.

Divide for right front

Row 1 1 tr (dc) in back lps of next 22 [23; 25; 26; 28; 29; 31] sts,
dec 1 tr (dc) over next 2 sts, 1 ch, turn.
Row 2 Dec 1 dc (sc) over next 2 sts, dc (sc) to end, 3 ch, turn.
Row 3 Tr (dc) in back loops to last 2 sts, 1 tr (dc) over next 2 sts,
1 ch, turn.

Figure 23 This zippered, shorter length jacket is suitable for man or woman

Work Rows 1 to 3 once then Row 2 once more.
Work a further 14 [14;14;14;16;16;16] rows in patt on remaining 20 [21;22;24;26;27;29] sts which should finish at neck edge. Ss (sl st) 6 [8;9;10;11;12;13]. Work 6 rows in patt on remaining sts. Break off yarn.

Back
Rejoin yarn to 11th st from right front armhole edge, 3 ch, dec 1 tr (dc) over next 2 sts, 37 [41;43;47;49;53;55] tr (dc) in back lps, dec 1 tr (dc) over next 2 sts, 1 ch, turn.
Work 4 rows patt, dec 1 st at each end of the row, then work 20 [20;20;20;22;22;22] rows in patt. Break off yarn.

Left front
Rejoin yarn to 11th st from back armhole edge, 3 ch, dec 1 tr (dc) over next 2 sts, tr (dc) in back lps to end, 1 ch, turn. Work 4 rows patt, dec 1 st at armhole edge. Work 16 [16;16;16;16;18;18;18] rows patt.
Next row Tr (dc) in back lp, on next 19 [20;21;23;25;26;28) sts, 1 ch, turn.
Work 5 rows in patt. Break off yarn.

Sleeves
Make 32 ch.

Foundation row 1 dc (sc) in 3rd ch from hook, dc (sc) to end.
Work 46 rows in patt, inc 1 st at each end on next and every 4th row until there are 55 sts.
Shape for armhole
Next row Ss (sl st) over 6 sts, dc (sc) to last 6 sts, 3 ch, turn. Dec 1 st at each end of next 8 rows keeping patt. Break off yarn.

Waist border
Row 1 Rejoin yarn into rem lp of foundation ch with ws of work facing, 3 ch, *dec 1 tr (dc) over next 2 sts, 4 tr (dc), rep from * to end, 3 ch, turn.
Row 2 *Miss 4 sts, round stem of next tr (dc) starting at the bottom of the stem and putting the sts just above each other — work 1 quad tr (tr tr) 1 tr tr (dtr) 1 dtr (tr) 1 tr (dc) all round same stem with 1 dc (sc) in top of same st, rep from * to end, 1 ch, turn.
Row 3 Behind the group of long trs worked on the previous row lie 4 trs (dcs) from the 1st row of the border, * tr (dc) in each tr (dc) of first row, 1 dc (sc) on dc (sc) of 2nd row, rep from * to end. Break off yarn.

Cuffs
As for waist borders. Finish with 1 row cr st worked on rs. Join shoulder seams.

Neck
Pick up sts that are a multiple of 6 plus 1 and work as for waist border. With rs facing work 1 row cr st round neck, fronts and waist. As well as neatening the edge it makes the insertion of the zip easier. Join sleeve seams. Insert sleeves into armholes.
Attach zip.

SECTION D

VARIATIONS ON CLOAK
a Replace the chains with double trebles (trebles) to give a denser cloak. Only two layers are then required.
b Using the original pattern use five cloaks each one longer than the other.
c Use more stitches and a smaller hook to give a denser fabric with more weight.
d Add a hood similar to the one for the dressing grown, (p. 33).
e Add a high stand-up collar and broad front bands in treble (double crochet) with buttons and buttonholes. It is important also to include specially designed holes at waist level to enable the hands to be used.

VARIATIONS ON SHAWL TOP
a Use a different colour for each of the 'shawls'.
b Use a different colour for the panels of cluster pattern.
c Make one shawl much longer, add fringe and use as a shawl.

VARIATIONS FOR THE ZIPPERED JACKET
a Work the textured design given for the bands in the patt in a different colour.
b Replace zip with a textured band for a box jacket.
c Use a flat fabric for the main part i.e. work the treble (double crochet) row picking up two loops instead of one. Then add two breast pockets and two waist pockets with or without zips to give a 'battle dress' style.
d Add a drawstring at waist and neck level and elastic at cuffs, to keep out the wind.

e Replace zip with front bands in double crochet (single crochet) to take buttons and buttonholes.

DISPROPORTIONATE FIGURES

If the figure for which the garment is being made is not of stock size, it may sometimes be useful to accommodate irregularities by a change in the size of hook, without altering the number of stitches or stitch pattern. For example, extra large or extra small hips, waist, bust, tops of arms, etc. can be worked following the pattern but with a change of hook size.

Another occasion on which a change of hook size is a good idea is when one shoulder blade is noticeably larger than another, or one side of the bust differs considerably from the other. Similarly it is not uncommon to have a waist at one side but not at the other and here again, to get a better fit, a change of hook size can be used. It should be stressed that this is not the method to use for the majority of shapings and that a difference of more than three hook changes in one pattern piece will alter the texture of the fabric to a noticeable degree, e.g. a 5.50mm (H) hook for main pattern, 6.00mm (J) for over bust and top of arms and a 7.00mm (K) for hips is the most that would be acceptable.

VII **Half Trebles**

SECTION A

HALF TREBLE (HALF DOUBLE CROCHET): (htr [hdc]): 2 chain to turn.

The half treble (half double crochet) has been left as the last basic stitch, because it does not conform to many of the guidelines given previously. It differs from the other stitches in the following respects:
a the top of the stitch has three strands lying closely together instead of the usual two. Any two strands can be picked up in working but for consistency make sure the same two strands are picked up on each stitch. Should the three strands be picked up when the hook is inserted, the crochet will spread widthways.
b At the start of a row work into the stitch at the base of the turning chain as though making an increase, otherwise there is an ugly hole and an irregular side edge.
c At the end of the row omit working into the turning chain to compensate for the 'increase stitch' at the beginning of the row.

To work a htr (hdc), yoh before inserting the hook under 2 strands of the st of the row below, yoh and draw this through to the front of the st, yoh once more and draw yarn through all 3 lps on the hook (*diagram 18*). One half treble (half double crochet) made.

The height of the half treble (half double crochet) is between that of a double crochet (single crochet) and a treble (double crochet), hence only two chains are needed to turn.

TO INCREASE
a   at the beginning of a row: the top of the st immediately below the turning ch has already been worked into, so it is preferable that 2 htr (hdc) be put in the next st rather than having 3 htr (hdc) (i.e. 2 htr (hdc) and the turning ch at the start of the row.
b   at the end of a row: work a htr (hdc) in the top of the turning ch.

TO DECREASE
a   at the beginning of a row: omit working into the st immediately below the turning ch.
b   at the end of a row: work to the last 3 sts (i.e. the 2 sts and the turning ch) yoh and insert into next st, yoh, draw through to the front (3 lps on hook), insert hook into next st (without putting the yoh 1st) yoh and draw through to front (4 lps on the hook), yoh and draw through all 4 lps.

Diagram 18

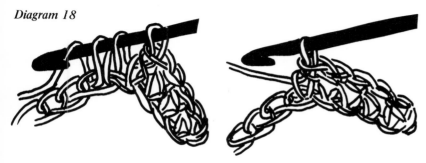

As the techniques for working the half treble (half double crochet) are slightly different than for other stitches, work a sample piece that includes some increasing and decreasing. Once more aran wool and a 5.00mm (H) hook are recommended, as this shows up the stitch construction clearly.

SECTION B

The half treble (half double crochet) being a law unto itself has characteristics that are quite different from the other basic crochet stitches. It is useful to experiment with the hook insertion as it gives many different effects.
   Try crocheting:
a   a piece of half treble (half double crochet) fabric where the front two strands are picked up one row and the back two strands are picked up on the returning row. This gives a different pattern on each side, (*figure 24a*).
b   Use the very last row of half treble (half double crochet) to form a frill by working a row of double crochet (single crochet) using only the front single strand of the stitch: a row of treble (double crochet) using the middle single strand and a row of double treble (treble) in the final back strand, of the last half treble (half double crochet) worked, (*figure 24b*).

a (front)

b

c

a (back)

Figure 24 a Half trebles (half double crochet) worked with one row picking up front two loops and next row picking up front two loops and the next row picking up back two loops to give a reversible fabric. Both sides shown here; b shows the last row used three times as an edging c picking up only one strand

c Try working one row half trebles (half double crochet) picking up only the very front lower strand and return along the next row picking up only the very back strand. The crochet will appear to have two rows of chain stitch embroidered on after the crochet was completed, (*figure 24c*).

SECTION C

A word of caution at this point for the inexperienced crocheter — the half-treble (half double crochet) is a tricky stitch so please make sure you fully understand sections A and B and have mastered the techniques before tackling the patterns in this section.

COVER UP (*figure 25*)

Materials
12 x 20g balls 4-ply acrylic (MS)
1 x 50g ball thick bouclé contrast (C)
7.00mm (K) hook.

Measurement
One size to fit from 81cm (32in) bust.

Tension (gauge)
5 sts to 5cm (2in)

Back
In MS and 7.00mm (K) hook make 37 ch.
Row 1 1 htr (hdc) into 3rd ch from hook, htr (hdc) to end, 2 ch, turn, (36 sts).
Work 16 rows htr (hdc).
Row 18 2 htr (hdc) in same place as turning ch, 2 htr (hdc) in next st, htr (hdc) to last 3 sts, 2 htr (hdc) in next st, 1 htr (hdc) in next st, 1 htr (hdc) in turning ch, 2 ch, turn.
Rep row 18, 8 times.
Row 27 htr (hdc) to end, 2 ch, turn, (72 sts).
Rep Row 27, 10 times. Fasten off yarn.

Border
Row 1 In C work a 'bee' st (i.e., 1 ss [sl st], 1 tr [dc]) round all

sides of the back, join with ss (sl st). Fasten off yarn.
Row 2 In MS dc (sc) to end, join with ss (sl st), 2 ch, turn,
(remember to put extra sts in at the corners as work must lie flat).
Row 3 *1 htr (hdc) in next st, work round this st that has just been
made as follows: (yoh, put hook in sp between last 2 sts made, yoh,
lp up by lifting hook to horizontal position) 3 times to give 7 lps,
yoh, draw through all 7 lps — one sideways puff stitch made. Miss 1
st, rep from * to end working last sideways puff st round the htr
(hdc) and the starting ch.
Rep rows 1 to 3 once.
Break off yarn.

Front

Work as for back to end of row 27. Work 11 rows htr (hdc) on 1st
32 sts, break off yarn. Work 11 rows htr (hdc) on last 32 sts. Break
off yarn.

Border

Work as for back but commence at base of neck and do not join into
rounds (*figure 25*).
    Make two ties. Attach one to each side of back piece at waist
level. The ties here are a length of chain with a crab stitch worked
into each chain.

Figure 25 Bikini cover-up relying on the edging for detail

BIKINI (*figure 26*)

Materials

3 balls 4-ply (MS)
1 ball thick bouclé contrast (C)
4.00mm (F) hook
90cm (36in) narrow elastic

Measurement

One size to fit 87cm (34in) bust but adjustments are made for a
larger or smaller figure in Section D.

Tension (gauge)

8 sts to 5cm (2in)

To work top

Cups (2 alike)
In MS and 4.00mm (F) hook make 3 ch, join with ss (sl st).
Rnd 1 2 ch, 8 htr (hdc) in ring, join with ss (sl st), 2 ch, turn.
Rnd 2 1 htr (hdc) in front lp of st in same place as turning ch, 2 htr
(hdc) in front lp of each st to end, join with ss (sl st), 2 ch, turn.
Rnd 3 3 htr (hdc) in back lp of st in same place as turning ch, *5 htr
(hdc) in back lps, 4 htr (hdc) in back lp of next st, rep from * once,
5 htr (hdc) in back lps, join with ss (sl st), 2 ch, turn.
Rnd 4 working in front lps only, 6 htr (hdc), *2 htr (hdc) in next st,
2 ch, 2 htr (hdc) in next st, 7 htr (hdc), rep from * once, 2 htr (hdc)
in next st, 2 ch, 2 htr (hdc) in next st, join with ss (sl st), 2 ch, turn.
Rnd 5 Working in back lps only, *2 htr (hdc) in next st, 3 ch, miss
1 htr (hdc) and 2 ch, 2 htr (hdc) in next st, 8 htr (hdc) rep from *
once, 2 htr (hdc) in next st, 3 ch, miss 1 htr (hdc) and 2 ch, 2 htr

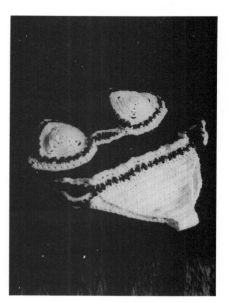

Figure 26 Bikini — in half-trebles (half double crochet) for sun worshippers

(hdc) in next st, 7 htr (hdc), join with ss (sl st), 2 ch, turn.

Rnd 6 Working in front lps only, 9 htr (hdc), miss 1 st, *7 htr (hdc) in 3 ch sp, 11 htr (hdc), miss 1 st, rep from * once, 7 htr (hdc) in 3 ch sp, 1 htr (hdc), join with ss (sl st).

Rnd 7 Working in back lps only 3 htr (hdc), *4 htr (hdc) in next st, 17 htr (hdc), rep from once, 4 htr (hdc) in next st, 13 htr (hdc), join with ss (sl st).

Rnd 8 Join in C and work in front lps only *1 tr (dc), miss 1 st, 1 ss (sl st), rep from * to end making last ss (sl st) join into a rnd. Break off contrast.

Rnd 9 In MS without turning work, 2 ch, *2 htr (hdc) in tr (dc), 1 htr (hdc) in ss (sl st), rep from * to end, join with ss (sl st), 2 ch, turn.

Rnd 10 Work sideways puff to end working last st round htr (hdc) and turning ch tog (as described in cover-up border).

To make front joining piece

9 ch in C, 1 tr (dc) in 4th ch from hook, *1 ss (sl st), 1 tr (dc), rep from * to last st, 1 ss (sl st) in last st. Break off C.

In MS work round both sides of bouclé in dc (sc) putting 5 dc (sc) in end sts. Follow this with 1 rnd sideways puff.

Make 4 ties in C with approx 50 ch, work 1 cr st in each ch.

To make up

Sew the pieces together using the main yarn as a sewing thread.

To work bikini bottom

In MS and 4.00m (F) hook make 35 ch.

Row 1 1 htr (hdc) in 3rd ch from hook, htr (hdc) to end, 2 ch, turn, (34 sts).

Row 2 htr (hdc) to end, 2 ch, turn.

Row 3 1 htr (hdc) in next st (not the same place as turning ch) htr (hdc) to end, (33 sts).

Rep row 3, 5 times.

Dec 1 st at each end of next 3 rows.

Dec 2 sts at each end of next 3 rows.

Work 6 rows straight.

Inc 2 sts at each end of next 4 rows.

Inc 1 st at each end of next 5 rows.

Work 14 rows straight.

Break off yarn.

Join C to last st made, 15 ch, join ch to front, break off yarn. Make another 15 ch in contrast to join other side of bikini, do not break off this yarn but continue round bikini hips with *1 ss (sl st), 1 tr (dc), rep from * to last st, join into a rnd with a ss (sl st). Break off yarn.

Work 1 row dc (sc) in M. Work a final row of sideways puff as described in cover-up border.

Sew narrow elastic to back of hip border.

SECTION D

VARIATIONS FOR THE COVER-UP

a Use a thick yarn but same hook and make as a winter poncho-style, outdoor blanket.

b Split front in half, join sides and have as an edge-to-edge cover-up.

c Join underarm seams and part of the side seams, leaving a split at hip level. Thread a narrow belt through the stitches at waist level.

d Use as a basis for an evening jacket threading narrow ribbon through the htr (hdc) rows. The best overall effect for this would be by incorporating the suggestion at **b**.

VARIATIONS FOR THE BIKINI

a Cups can be made larger by working the border round each cup two or even three times.

b The ties can be made in the same way as the centre joining strap.

c When the techniques in Chapter VIII have been mastered other triangular patterns in different stitches can be utilized.

d Broad ribbon and/or elastic can be used instead of the crochet borders.

DESIGNING USING DRESSMAKER'S PAPER PATTERNS

To incorporate additional shape, and style into the designing of garments, dressmaker's patterns can be used. Modification to these will be necessary and listed below are some points to be taken into consideration when working from these patterns.

a Choose a pattern that fits and flatters the figure

b Cut away the seam allowance on each pattern piece

c Ideally choose a pattern without many darts

d Ignore the darts in a skirt pattern and make the final waistband on a size smaller hook.

e In the majority of cases it is best to close the darts in the bodice pattern and redraw this new shape on another piece of paper (see Chapter IX, Section D for the working in of darts as the pattern progresses).

f Join side seams together and work bodice fronts and back as one piece, wherever possible.

g For a fitted sleeve, draw a very gentle, shallow curve from one point of easing to the other point of easing and follow this new line. There is no real need to have such a deep sleeve head in a crochet fabric as there is in a woven fabric or to have the sleeve obviously eased into the armhole. NB: do not allow the sleeve head to be *stretched* into the armhole as this will be noticeable and look ugly, as well as being restrictive in movement to the wearer.

h Add 1 cm (½in) extra at the side seam of a fitted sleeve.

i Work a tension (gauge) piece to calculate stitches.

j Make crochet the same size as the adjusted paper pattern plus an allowance of one stitch at each side for joinings.

k Always measure work on a flat table with nothing under the paper pattern. Do not stretch or squash the crochet during the measuring but allow it to lie on the pattern naturally.

l Hang heavy coats and skirt panels before the final make up, so that the weight of the yarn will drop to its natural level *before* wearing.

m Follow the guidelines given in Chapter IX, Section D for borders, collars, cuffs, waist fittings etc.

VIII Circles and Tubes

SECTION A

TUBES

These are made by joining each row of crochet together with a ss (sl st) to form a tube and are called rounds (rnd). Turning chs are made in the same way as in flat, straight sided, fabrics when a new row is started. It is suggested that the work is turned at the beginning of each round as it is easier to keep the position of the joins in a straight line. If the same side of the tube is always kept facing the crochet worker, the joins will be at an angle (*figure 27*).

Figure 27 Tubular crocheting **a** with same side facing rows 2-4, first stitch is worked in same place as turning chain; rows 5-9, first stitch is placed in the next st; **b** work is turned on every row

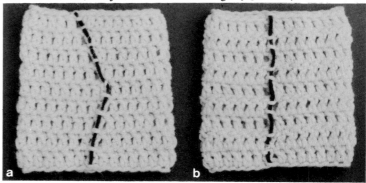

CIRCLES

Circles are usually made from the centre outwards. The rounds are joined together with a ss (sl st). Most motifs start out as circles even if the final shape is to be octagon, hexagon, square, etc.

The circumference of the circle increases on every round, thus requiring extra stitches for every row. It is the circumference that must lie flat at all stages of its production, if a flat motif is to result.

There are many factors to take into consideration when making circles. For example, thickness of the yarn and hook can alter the number of stitches required. The following table is a stitch quide to the number of increases needed in each row and is found to work in most instances when 4-ply; double knitting (worsted) and aran wools are used on the middle range of hook sizes, i.e. 3.5mm (E) for 4-ply; 4.50mm (F) or 5.00mm (H) for double knitting (worsted) and 5.00mm (H) or 6.00 mm (I) for aran.

In addition to the stitch guide below consider the following points:
a In a circle of trebles (double crochet) it is necessary to increase

Start with 4 ch joined by ss (sl st)				
Into the ring work:	6 dc (sc)	8 htr (hdc)	12 tr (dc)	24 dtr (tr)
Join with ss (sl st), 1 ch. Turn work.				
Work 2 sts of the same kind in each st				
This gives an inc per rnd of	6 dc (sc)	8 htr (hdc)	12 tr (dc)	24 dtr (tr)
Inc on each rnd by	6 dc (sc)	8 htr (hdc)	12 tr (dc)	24 dtr (tr)

by 12 stitches on every round which is exactly twice as many increased stitches per round as is needed for the double crochet (single crochet). The reason is that the treble (double crochet) stitch is twice as tall as the double crochet (single crochet) stitch and the tops of the trebles (double crochet) have to cover a larger area than the tops of the double crochet (single crochet).

Two rounds of double crochet (single crochet) are as tall as one round of treble (double crochet) and at the end of working two rounds of double crochet (single crochet) there is the same number of stitches as one round of treble.

b Should the type of stitch to be used on each round change, use the table given above to help decide how many increases are required. For example, in a circle made of double trebles (trebles) but with a round of double crochet (single crochet) included occasionally, on the rounds of double treble (treble) increase by 24 stitches per round, but on the double crochet (single crochet) round only six extra stitches should be made.

c To see exactly where a round starts use either a piece of coloured thread or a safety pin to mark where the work commenced. This can be moved upwards in large motifs.

d Turning the work on each round is optional but it is generally easier to keep the correct number of stitches if this is done, and also the position of the joins remains in a straight line, not slantingly following the natural stitch bias. In addition, the increases do not sit on top of each other which simplifies the task when working a true circle.

e After working two or three rounds, place the circle on a flat smooth surface and check that it is really lying flat. It really doesn't pay to cheat by trying to pull or stretch it or trying to squash it flat. The faults only get worse as the work progresses. If it seems to frill there are too many stitches in the last round so pull the work back and make less increases per round. If the work curls up into a cup shape, there are not enough stitches being incorporated, so start the circle again and use more stitch increases than before.

f When making circles for the first time there is a tendency to put all the increases in the same place. What actually happens if this is done, is to work straight rows of crochet between points. This kind of increasing does not give a curve, so a circle of double crochet (single crochet) produces hexagons (*figure 28a*), a circle of half trebles (half double crochet) produces octagons (*figure 28b*), and so on. Squares are 'circles' with the increases divided into four and then

*Figure 28 Circles **a** hexagon in double crochet (single crochet)*
Figure 28b octagon in half trebles (half double crochet)
Figure 28c a square

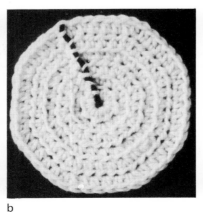

a b c

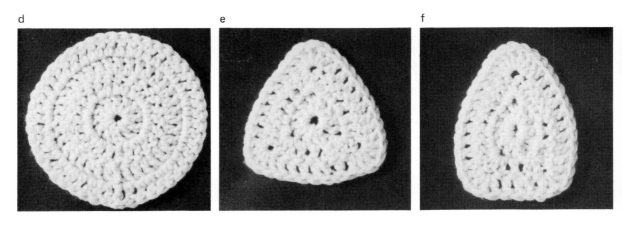

d   e   f

Figure 28d *a true circle*
Figures 28e and f *triangles*

worked at four equal points in the circle (*figure 28c*). For example, a square of half trebles (half double crochet) has four points where two extra stitches are made (i.e. htr [hdc] in the corner sts).
g True circles can only be achieved if the place where the increases take place are changed on each round (*figure 28d*).

To put these guidelines into practice try making for yourself: a true circle; a hexagon of double crochet (single crochet); an octagon of half treble (half double crochet); a 'cup' shape using less increases each round; a full frilly circle by using more increases each round.

SECTION B

Tubes can be utilized as covers for many items of household furnishings and also used in fashion. For instance, the fingers of a glove fit more comfortably when worked as tubes with the stitches drawn together at the tip. Seamless garments are particularly flattering and comfortable to certain types of figure.

Try making belts of tubes by plaiting together long narrow crocheted tubes of different colours and by padding a long crocheted tube and then knotting it to contain the padding into sections. It is not always possible to get a belt to match exactly a garment that has been made, but if a tube of crochet is made from the same yarn as the garment just wide enough to cover a stiff leather or plastic belt that is no longer looking its best, the firmness of the belt will keep the crochet in place. (If the original belt is a strong contrast to the colour of the crochet it might be necessary to wrap the belt in a piece of cloth that is similar in colour to the yarn being used in the crochet, or alternatively use it as a design feature and work a lacy design into the covering tube.)

With the guidelines given in Section A for circles plus your own experience gained by practising the ideas given, try producing the following;
a covered items such as buttons. A hint for making firm buttons is to use a hook at least two sizes smaller so that the finished work is stiff and rigid just the kind of crochet that is not wanted in the actual garment.
b A fabric containing lots of even-sized circles which have been sewn or crocheted together in rows. Try to avoid including half circles as these tend to pull out of shape.

c A fabric of triangles using the right number of increases for the stitch being used on each round, but only in three places, (*figure 28e* and *f*).

d A fabric made up of squares which are particularly useful for large heavy items such as full length ponchos, heavy coats, etc., as each square is not heavy to work by itself but when they are joined together, the work could be cumbersome to handle.

A larger hole can be made in the centre of a motif by starting with a foundation chain which has the same number of chains as would have been stitches of the row below, e.g., omitting five rows of treble (double crochet) the number of chain needed is five (rows) times 12 (stitches) = 60 (chain). This is how the stitches for the collar were calculated.

SECTION C

It is not necessary to turn the work after every row in crochet. This is a particular advantage when working in colours using one colour for only one row at a time.

The following pattern is a good example of this method of crochet as the work is only turned on every other row when the threads of the two yarns are at the same side. Leave the loop of the first yarn in a safety pin and catch it into the last stitch of the second yarn when it is eventually worked. Slip stitch the yarn up the stem of the row just worked and then crochet the pattern in the usual way.

CIRCULAR (BUTTON-THROUGH) OVERTOP (*figure 29*)

Materials
6 balls Main shade in Argyll Finesse mohair
5 balls Contrast in Argyll Finesse mohair
9.00mm (wood 15) and 4.50mm (G) hooks.
7 buttons

Measurement
To fit bust size 77-91cm (30-36in)

Tension (gauge)
4 dtr (tr) to 7cm (2¾in)

To make
Work 31 ch in MS using 9.00mm (wood 15) hook.
Row 1 1 tr (dc) in 4th ch from hook, *2 tr (dc) in next ch, 1 tr (dc) in next ch, rep from * to last st, 1 tr (dc) in last st, (42 sts).
Row 2 In C, 4 ch, turn, *1 dtr (tr), 1 dtr (tr) 2 ch 1 dtr (tr) in next st, rep from * to end. Do not turn work.
Row 3 In M, 4 ch, 1 dtr (tr), *1 dtr (tr) 2 ch 1 dtr (tr) in ch sp, 1 dtr (tr), rep from * to last st, 1 dtr (tr) in last st.
Row 4 In C, 4 ch, turn, 2 dtr (tr), *1 ch 1 dtr (tr) in ch sp, 2 dtr (tr), 1 dtr (tr) 2 ch 1 dtr (tr) in ch sp, rep from * to last 3 sts, 3 dtr (tr). Do not turn work.
Row 5 In MS as Row 4. Turn work.

Figure 29   *Circular, button-through overtop*

Row 6 In C, 4 ch, 3 dtr (tr), 1 dtr (tr) in ch sp, *3 dtr (tr), 1 dtr (tr) 2 ch 1 dtr (tr) in ch sp, rep from * to last 4 sts, 4 dtr (tr). Do not turn work.

Row 7 As Row 6 in MS. Turn work.

Row 8 In C, 4 ch, 4 dtr (tr) in ch sp, *4 dtr (tr), 1 dtr (tr) 2 ch 1 dtr (tr) in ch sp, rep from * to last 5 sts, 5 dtr (tr). Do not turn work.

Row 9 In MS as Row 8. Turn work.

Row 10 In C, 4 ch, 5 dtr (tr), 1 dtr (tr) 2 ch 1 dtr (tr) in ch sp, *5 dtr (tr), 1 dtr (tr) 2 ch 1 dtr (tr) in ch sp, rep from * to last 6 sts, 6 dtr (tr). Do not turn work.

Row 11 In MS as Row 10. Turn work.

Row 12 In C, 4 ch, *6 dtr (tr), 1 dtr (tr) 2 ch 1 dtr (tr) in ch sp, rep from * to last 7 sts, 7 dtr (tr). Do not turn work.

Row 13 In MS as Row 12. Turn work.

Row 14 In C, 4 ch, 7 dtr (tr), 1 dtr (tr) 2 ch 1 dtr (tr) *7 dtr (tr), 1 dtr (tr) 2 ch 1 dtr (tr) in ch sp, rep from * to last 8 sts, 8 dtr (tr). Do not turn work.

Break off C.

Row 15 In MS, 4 ch, 8 dtr (tr), 1 dtr (tr) 2 ch 1 dtr (tr) in ch sp, *8 dtr (tr), 1 dtr (tr) 2 ch 1 dtr (tr) in ch sp, rep from * to last 9 sts, 9 dtr (tr).

Front and neck border

With 4.50mm (G) hook work dc (sc) up right front, put 3 dc (sc) in each row and 3 dc (sc) in corner st, 2 dc (sc) in each ch of neck, 3 dc (sc) in corner st, 3 dc (sc) in each row down left front.

Work 2 rows dc (sc) putting 3 dc (sc) in each corner st.

Mark position of 6 buttons on left front. Work 1 row dc (sc) making buttonholes to correspond to marks by missing 1 st and replacing it with 1 ch. Work 2 rows dc (sc).

Cuffs

Fold circle in half for centre back and mark points for sleeves by counting 28 dtr (tr). Use next 14 dtr (tr) for cuffs (check numbers are even on both sides of garment). Join in MS with 4.50mm (G) hook. Work 1 dc (sc) in each dtr (tr) and 2 dc (sc) in ch sp. Join with ss (sl st). Work 4 rows dc (sc). Break off yarn. Work other sleeve cuff to match.

Join underarm seams on ws taking 18 dtr (tr) which should end in a 2 ch sp.

With rs facing and 4.50mm (G) hook rejoin MS to base of left front band. 1 ch, 4 dc (sc) across band, 2 dc (sc) in each dtr (tr) and 4 dc (sc) in ch sp along remaining sts, 5 dc (sc) across right band.

Work 5 rows dc (sc) making a button-hole on 3rd row at base of lh border.

Break off yarn.
Attach buttons.

EVENING TOP OF CIRCLES (*figure 30*)

Materials
8 balls Robin Bambino 4-ply
4.00mm (F) hook
Matching shirring elastic

Measurement
To fit bust size 82-87cm (32-34in)

Tension (gauge)
Centre diameter of a border circle = 5cm (2in)

Main piece
158 ch

Row 1 1 dc (sc) in 2nd ch from hook, 3 dc (sc), miss 3 ch, 3 tr (dc) in next st *miss 3 ch, 1 dc (sc) in next st, miss 3 ch, 3 tr (dc) in next st, 5 ch, 1 dc (sc) in 2nd ch from hook, 3 dc (sc), miss 3 ch, 3 tr (dc) in same place as last 3 tr (dc) rep from * 17 times, miss 3 ch, 1 dc (sc), 4 ch, turn.

Row 2 Insert hook into base of 4 ch, yoh, draw through to front and lp 2cm (¾in) (insert hook in next st, yoh, draw through to front and lp 2cm ¾in]) 7 times, yoh, and draw through all the lps, 3 ch, *1 dc (sc) in next st, 3 ch, 1 2cm (¾in) lp in next 15 sts, yoh, draw through all 16 lps, 3 ch, rep from * to last st, 1 dc (sc), 1 ch, turn (*figure 31*).

Row 3 1 dc (sc) on dc (sc) *3 tr (dc) in centre of gr, 5 ch, miss 1 st, 4 dc (sc), 3 tr (dc) in same place as 3 tr (dc), miss 3 ch, 1 dc (sc) in next st, rep from * to last ½ gr, 3 tr (dc) in centre of ½ gr, 8 ch, turn.

Row 4 *1 2cm (¾in) lp in 4th ch from hook and in next 14 sts, yoh, draw through all 16 lps, 3 ch, 1 dc (sc) in next st, 3 ch, rep from * to ½ gr. 1 2cm (¾in) lp in next 8 sts, yoh, draw through all lps, 9 ch, turn.

Rep rows 1-4 twice and rows 1 and 2 once.

Neck and shoulder border circles
24 ch, join with ss (sl st).
With rs facing 3 ch, 41 tr (dc) in 24 ch sp, join with ss (sl st), turn work.
With ws facing *1 tr (dc), 1 ss (sl st), rep from * to end. Break off yarn.

Figure 30 Dainty top of interlocking rings and sunburst design, suitable for day or evening

Figure 31 Close up of the fabric which continues the theme of a circle throughout the top

Make another ring but link 24 ch with the ss (sl st) after slipping it through the first completed ring.

Make a further 17 rings this way.

19th ring Link the starting chain into 1st and last ring.

NB: There is a rs and a ws to the rings, make sure they are all lying flat with the same sides upwards before closing the final ring.

Centre front and waist circles

Make the 20th ring and link it into any one of the circles in the neck and shoulder border so that it drops down at right angles.

Attach a further 13 rings to make a T-shape and link these into the 23rd ring to form an I-shape with 3 free circles at centre front.

St circles firmly together and connect the main piece of crochet fabric to form a tube. There should be 6 free circles for a single shoulder strap and no circles at the underarm.

If necessary, shirring elastic can be inserted round bust for added security.

COLLAR (*figure 32*)

Materials
Coats 20s mercerized cotton
1.50mm (10) hook
2 buttons
ribbon (optional)

Measurement
One size to fit average neck.

To make
144 ch

Row 1 1 dc (sc) in 3rd st from hook, dc (sc) to end. Do not turn work.

Row 2 *4 cr sts miss 1 st rep from * to end, 1 ss (sl st) down side of dc (sc) row.

Row 3 Working into foundation ch again: 4 ch, *2 dtr (tr), 3 ch miss 2 ch, 2 dtr (tr), 3 ch miss 3 ch, rep from * to end, (31 sps, finishing with miss 2 ch), 1 ch, turn.

Row 4 1 dc (sc) in each dtr (tr), 3 dc (sc) in each sp but with 4 dc (sc) in every 5th sp (164 sts), 4 ch, turn.

Row 5 1 dtr (tr), *5 ch miss 1 ch, 1 tr (dc), (5 ch miss 2 ch, 1tr [dc]) 4 times, 5 ch, miss 1 ch, 3 dtr (tr), rep from * to end but finish with 2 dtr (tr), 4 ch, turn.

Row 6 1 tr (dc) in same place, 1 RdtrF (RtrF) *(miss 1 lp, 5 ch, 1 dc [sc] in next 1p) 4 times, 5 ch, 1 RdtrF (RtrF), 1 ch, 1 tr (dc) in sp, 1 ch, 1 RdtrF (RtrF), 1 ch, 1 tr (dc), 1 ch, 1 RdtrF (RtrF), rep from * to end omitting last ch, 1 RdtrF (RtrF), 4 ch, turn.

Row 7 (1 tr [dc] 1 ch in sp) twice, RdtrB (RtrB) *(5ch, 1 dc [sc] in lp) 3 times, 5 ch, 1 RdtrB (RtrB), 1 ch (1 tr [dc] in sp, 1 ch, 1 tr [dc] in sp, 1 ch, 1 RdtrB [RtrB], 1 ch) twice, rep from * working last bracket once only at end, 4 ch, turn.

Row 8 1 tr 1 ch in each of next 3 sps, 1 RdtrF (RtrF) *(6 ch, 1 dc [sc] in lp) twice, 6 ch, 1 RdtrF (RtrF), 1 ch (1 tr [dc], 1 ch in each of next 3 sps, 1 RdtrF [RtrF], 1 ch) twice, rep from * to end working last bracket once only at end, 4 ch, turn.

Figure 32 Collar based on the principle of a circle p. 64-5

Row 9 1 tr (dc) 1 ch in next 4 sps, 1 RdtrB (RtrB) *7 ch, 1 dc (sc) in lp, 7 ch (1 RdtrB [RtrB] , 1 ch 1 tr [dc] in next 4 sps) twice, 1 ch, 1 RdtrB (RtrB) to end working brackets once only at end, 4 ch, turn.
Row 10 1 tr (dc) 1 ch in next 5 sps, 1 RdtrF (RtrF) *5 ch, 1 dc (sc) in dc (sc), 5 ch, (1 RdtrF [RtrF] , 1 ch 1 tr in next 5 sps) twice, 1 ch, 1 RdtrF (RtrF) rep from * to end working brackets once only at end, 4 ch, turn.
Row 11 1 tr (dc) in next 6 sps, 1 RdtrB (RtrB), *2 ch 1 RdtrB (RtrB) round dc (sc) 2 rows below 2 ch, (1 RdtrB [RtrB] , 1 ch 1 tr (dc) in next 6 sps) twice, 1 ch 1 RdtrB (RtrB) to end, only work brackets once to finish, 4 ch, turn.
Row 12 3 tr (dc) in sp immediately below, miss 1 tr (dc), 1 ss (sl st) in next tr (dc), *miss 2 tr (dc), 7 tr (dc) in next sp, miss 2 tr (dc), 1 ss (sl st) in next dtr (tr), 4 tr (dc) 1 RdtrF (RtrF) 4 tr (dc) in next Rdtr (Rtr), 1 ss (sl st) in next Rdtr (Rtr), miss 2 tr (dc), 7 tr (dc) in next sp, miss 2 tr (dc), 1 ss (sl st) in next Rdtr (Rtr), miss 1 tr (dc), 4 tr (dc) 1 RdtrF (RtrF) 4 tr (dc) in next Rdtr (Rtr), miss 1 tr (dc), 1 ss (sl st) in next tr (dc), rep from * to last 7 sps, miss 2 tr (dc), 7 tr (dc) in next sp, miss 2 tr (dc), 1 ss (sl st) in next tr (dc), miss 2 tr (dc), 4 tr (dc) in top of turning ch. Continue by working down side edge of collar with 26 dc (sc).
One row cr st on side edge. Break off.
Rejoin cotton to other side edge with rs of collar facing and work 1 row dc (sc), (26 sts). Work 1 row cr st, putting 2 5-ch lps for buttons at the same level as the 2 dc rows of main part of collar. Break off yarn.

SECTION D

VARIATIONS FOR THE CIRCULAR TOP

a Use one colour only

b Omit cuffs and waist bands. Put one row double crochet (single crochet) at end and wear as a cape.

c Omit buttonholes. Replace double crochet (single crochet) with one row treble (double crochet) and thread ribbon or cord through cuffs, waist and neck for ties.

d Make top as an unbroken circle with a slightly larger neck size and wear as a sweater or overtop.

e Use this pattern as an alternative to the cloak pattern on p. 51.

VARIATIONS FOR THE EVENING TOP OF CIRCLES

a Make top strapless, using 16 circles instead of 21.

b If the three circles at centre front are a little daring omit them. Make the main piece large enough to join into a tube for a solid front.

c Add another strap of six circles.

d Use very broad ribbon to thread through the circles.

e Back with a contrasting coloured material.

VARIATIONS FOR THE COLLAR

a Use fine nylon press studs as a fastener instead of buttons.

b Omit the velvet ribbon.

c Use ribbon as a tie and complete fastenings with a small hook and eye hidden beneath the bow.

d Extend the neckband so that it can be stitched inside a dress and turned over to the right side to lie flat but free.

e Use same pattern to make matching cuffs.

DESIGNS WITHOUT SEAMS

Baby clothes, bedjackets, garments for tender skin, are more comfortable if there are no seams. Joinings in lacy stitch patterns are very noticeable and if these can be worked 'in the round' they will keep their ethereal look and give the garment a professional touch. To achieve a seamless garment, the crochet is worked up or down rather than sideways. Working upwards in a dress or sweater, make a tube for the body to reach the underarm using the hip or bust measure; whichever is the larger. Make two tubes for the sleeves. Work a yoke on a decreasing circle principle using the stitches of the sleeves and body piece (*diagram 19*). Alternatively, start with the yoke and work downwards.

Cardigans, jackets and coats can be made seamless by working the two fronts and the back, separately from the neck, down to just below the armholes; then working the rest of the garment in one. Sleeves can be worked down to the cuff. The first row commences with the stitches of the armhole of the fronts and back.

Skirts are quite simple to work in a tubular form even though increasing is necessary to get a good fit. Once again it is advised that the crochet is worked downwards and hung. It is possible to have as little as four increase points on a crochet skirt but this will make the hemline poke out quite noticeably. Even the six panel skirt in Chapter III, Section C has a definite A-line look. To avoid this and to get a softer line use more increase points.

Trousers can be worked in a tube from the waist (or hip) down to the crotch. The legs can then be worked in tubes, increasing and decreasing for fit as necessary.

Mittens, gloves, socks and legwarmers can be uncomfortable during wearing if there is a seam, particularly socks which rub against both foot and shoe.

The main thing to remember when working without seams is to check that the row joins are in a straight line.

IX Shaping

SECTION A

INCREASING AND DECREASING

Many patterns can be made by working a large number of stitches in one place and then removing them on the same row in another place. Increases cause the row to be distorted giving it a pointed or scalloped look at the top of the row i.e. an upward thrust. Decreasing also creates a similar distortion and pushes the level of the row downwards (*figures 33a and b*).

CHEVRONS

If you have a logical mind chevrons are not a problem once it is understood that two extra stitches are added to the one stitch at the top of a peak and three stitches are drawn together to make one stitch in the hollows. Edges of chevrons can cause confusion to some people, but if it is remembered that the turning chains and first stitch count as just one stitch at the beginning of the row and if at the same time it is remembered that the three single stitches are

Figure 33a and b   shaping by increasing and decreasing

a

b

71

always three single stitches and do not ever reduce to two or increase to four, the sides will remain straight.

TO MAKE CHEVRONS USING TREBLES (DOUBLE CROCHET)

Work a length of ch that divides by 10 with 1 left over plus 2 further ch for turning.

Foundation Row 1 tr (dc) in 4th ch from hook, *3 tr (dc), 3 tr (dc) in next ch, 3 tr (dc), (yoh, insert hook *into next ch*, yoh, draw to front, yoh, draw through 2 lps) 3 times, yoh, draw through all 4 lps — one three treble cluster (double cluster) made. Rep from * to last 9 ch, 3 tr (dc), 3 tr (dc) in next st, 3 tr (dc), (yoh, insert hook *into next ch*, yoh, draw through to front, yoh, draw through 2 lps) twice yoh, draw through the 3 lps on hook — one three treble cluster (double crochet cluster), 3 ch, turn.

Patt row 4 tr (dc), *3 tr (dc) in next st, 3 tr (dc), 1 3trcl (3dccl), 3 tr (dc), rep from * to last 5 sts, 3 tr (dc) in next st, 3 tr (dc), 1 2trcl (dccl), 3 ch, turn.

NB: The turning chain is not used as a stitch at the end of the row as the 1st tr (dc) of a row and the turning ch count as a 2trcl (dccl).

INCREASING

Put 5 tr (dc), instead of 3 in the centre st of the point on one row, and then continue with patt as usual. There will be 1 extra tr (dc) on each side between the point and the hollow. If the chevrons are being worked in a thick yarn, work the incs in over 2 rows. The patt of the skirt uses this last method.

SECTION B

Chevrons can be produced by using chain stitches for the inceases or by missing stitches for the decreases. To obtain this variation of the pattern substitute '1 tr (dc), 1 ch, 1 tr (dc) in next st' for '3 tr (dc) in next st', and substitute 'miss 1 st, 1 tr (dc) in next st, miss 1 st' for the '3 trcl (dccl)'. A further variation of chevrons is to be found in the skirt pattern below. Try for yourself different ways of producing chevrons.

STITCH HEIGHTS

Scallops and points can be made by using the heights of the various stitches to create shape. This method is particularly useful for the petals of flowers, a scalloped edge or shell edge, and also to shape a garment at the shoulders and bust darts (see Section D).

When chevrons are worked onto a straight row as in the case of the skirt pattern, there has to be some method of making a row that fills in the gaps between the plain crochet and the chevron pattern. The use of stitch heights provides the answer. A section of crochet worked in plain rows followed by the chevron pattern as given in Section A, requires a row of crochet that will adjust the pattern. In this instance it is 2 ss (sl st), *1 dc (sc), 1 htr (hdc), 1 tr (dc), 1 dtr (tr), 1 tr (dc), 1 htr (hdc), 1 dc (sc), 3 ss (sl st), rep from * to end but finishing with only 2 ss (sl st) instead of 3 ss (sl st).

The following pattern in two colours clearly shows the use of stitch heights to create shape within a fabric (*figure 33c*).

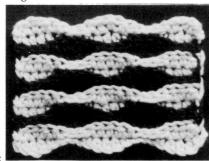

Figure 33c *shaping by using stitch heights*

c

RIPPLE PATTERN

Make a ch of 22 sts in MS.

Row 1 1 htr (hdc) in 3rd ch from hook, 2 htr (hdc), 1 dc (sc), *3 ss (sl st), 1 dc (sc), 3 htr (hdc), 1 dc (sc), rep from * once, 1 ch.

Row 2 Working under 2 strands as normal *3 htr (hdc), 1 dc (sc), 3 ss (sl st), 1 dc (sc), rep from * once, 3 htr (hdc), 1 dc (sc), 1 ch.

Row 3 In C and *working into the back lps only* *3 ss (sl st), 1 dc (sc), 3 htr (hdc), 1 dc (sc), rep from * once, 3 ss (sl st), 1 dc (sc), 1 ch.

Row 4 In C and under 2 lps *3 ss (sl st), 1 dc (sc), 3 htr (hdc), 1 dc (sc), rep from * once, 3 ss (sl st), 1 dc (sc), 1 ch.

Row 5 In MS and *under back lp only* *3 htr (hdc), 1 dc (sc), 3 ss (sl st), 1 dc (sc), rep from * once, 3 htr (hdc), 1 dc (sc), 1 ch.

Rows 2-5 form the pattern. Rep these 4 rows until the required length is reached.

Another example of the use of stitch heights to create shape is in the actual stitch pattern of the summer top given in Section C below.

SECTION C

UNISEX PULLOVER (*figure 34*)

Progressive decreasing at the armhole edge gives a round armhole instead of the angular ones used in most of the patterns so far. The use of a crochet rib helps to draw the armhole bands onto the figure. It is vital that the mitre shaping of the 'V' neck is accurately done as the pattern is so plain that the eye is automatically drawn to the mitre and any errors will be obvious.

Materials
4 balls Sirdar Chenille
2 balls Sirdar Majestic DK (worsted)
4.00mm (F) and 7.00mm (K) hooks

Measurement
To fit bust/chest size 92-97cm (36-38in)

Tension (gauge)
7 sts to 9cm (3½in) worked in chenille

Back
Foundation chain make 43 ch with 7.00mm (K) hook and chenille.
Row 1 1 tr (dc) in 4th ch from hook, tr (dc) to end, 3 ch, turn, (41 sts).
Work 15 rows tr (dc).
Next row ss (sl st) over 5 sts, 3 ch, tr (dc) next 2 sts tog, 26 tr (dc), tr (dc) next 2 sts tog, 3 ch, turn†.
Next row tr (dc) 2 tog, 26 tr (dc), tr (dc) next 2 sts tog, 3 ch, turn.
Work 12 rows on the remaining 29 sts.

Front
Work as back until †
Next row tr (dc) 2 tog, 11 tr (dc), tr (dc) tr (dc) 2 tog, 3 ch, turn.
Next row tr (dc) 2 tog, tr (dc) to the end, 3 ch, turn.
Next row tr (dc) to last 2 sts, tr (dc) 2 tog, 3 ch, turn.

Figure 34 *Classic V neck pullover suitable for male or female*

73

Continue keeping armhole edge straight and decreasing 1 st at neck edge on every alternate row.

Work other side to match reversing all shapings. Join shoulder and side seams.

Waistband

With 4.00mm (F) hook and DK (worsted) work 1 row tr (dc) into foundation ch of Chenille making 5 DK (worsted) trs (dc) for every 3 Chenille trs (dc). Work 5 rows Rtr (Rdc) rib. (p. 41) Fasten off yarn.

Armhole Bands

Make 76 trs (dc) evenly around armhole edge. Work 3 rows Rtr (Rdc) rib. Fasten off yarn.

Neckband

Commence at centre back neck and make 100 tr (dc) evenly round neck edge ensuring there is a single tr (dc) in the unworked Chenille tr (dc) at centre front and working the 2 trs (dc) tog immediately prior to the central strand and 2 tr (dc) tog immediately after the central strand.

Work 1 row Rtr (Rdc) rib but take care that the central front tr (dc) has its ridge to the front on the rs of the work, and tr (dc) 3 tog on either side of this st.

Work 1 row Rtr (Rdc) rib but working 1 RtrF (RdcF) round the stems of the 2 tr (dc) (prior to the central st of the 'V' shaping tog). Work the central st on its own and work 1 RtrF (RdcF) round stems of the next 2 tr (dc) tog.

This process should give you a neat mitred 'V' neck band. Rep these 2 rows if necessary.

CHEVRON SKIRT (*figure 21*)

Materials

15 (17; 19. 22) balls Falcon Llama 4-ply
4.00mm (F) hook
Elastic for waistband
15cm (6in) zip.

Measurement

To fit waist size 66 [71; 76; 81] cm (26 [28; 30; 32] in)

Tension (gauge)

4 sts to 2cm (¾in)

Skirt (2 pieces alike)

Make 80 [86; 92; 98] ch.
Row 1 1 dc (sc) in 3rd ch from hook, dc (sc) to end, 1 ch, turn.
Work 11 rows dc (sc) finishing with 3 ch, turn.
Row 13 1 row tr (dc), 3 ch, turn.
Row 14 1 tr (dc) in same place, 2trcl (2dccl), *1 RtrF (RdcF), 2trcl (2dccl), 3 tr (dc) in next st, 2trcl (2dccl), rep from * 11 [12; 13; 14] 13; 14] times, *RtrF (RdcF), 2trcl (2dccl), 2 tr (dc) in last st, 3 ch, turn (*figure 35*).

Row 15 As Row 14 but working Rtr (Rdc) back instead of front.
Row 16 (inc row) 1 tr (dc) in same place, 2 tr (dc), *1 RtrF (RdcF),
2 tr (dc), 3 tr (dc) in next st, 2 tr (dc), rep from * 11 [12; 13; 14]
times, *RtrF (RdcF), 2 tr (dc), 2 tr (dc) in last st, 3 ch, turn.
Row 17 1 tr (dc) in same place, 1 tr (dc), 2trcl (2dccl), *1 RtrB
(RdcB), 2trcl (2dccl), 1 tr (dc), 2 tr (dc) in next st, 1 tr (dc), 2trcl
(2dccl), rep from * 11 [12; 13; 14] times, 1 RtrB (RdcB), 2trcl
(2dccl), 1 tr (dc), 2 tr (dc) in last st, 3 ch, turn.
Rep row 17, 6 times alternating raised tr (dc) from front to back.
Row 24 (inc row) 1 tr (dc) in same place, 3 tr (dc), *1 RtrF (RdcF),
3 tr (dc), 3 tr (dc) in next st, 3 tr (dc), rep from * 11 [12; 13; 14]
times, 1 RtrF (RdcF), 3 tr (dc), 2 tr (dc) in next st, 3 ch, turn.
Row 25 1 tr (dc) in same place, 2 tr (dc), 2trcl (2dccl), *RtrB
(RdcB), 2trcl (2dccl), 2 tr (dc), 3 tr (dc) in next st, 2 tr (dc), 2trcl
(2dccl), rep from * 11 [12; 13; 14] times, 1 RtrB (RdcB), 2trcl
(2dccl), 2 tr (dc), 2 tr (dc) in last st, 3 ch, turn.
Rep Row 25, 12 times keeping Rtr (Rdc) on rs of work.
Row 38 (inc row) 1 tr (dc) in same place, 4 tr (dc), *1 RtrF (RdcF),
4 tr (dc), 3 tr (dc) in next st, 4 tr (dc), rep from * 11 [12; 13; 14]
times 1 RtrF (RdcF), 4 tr (dc), 2 tr (dc) in last st, 3 ch, turn.
Row 39 1 tr (dc) in same place, 3 tr (dc), 2trcl (2dccl), *1 RtrB
(RdcB), 2trcl (2dccl), 3 tr (dc), 3 tr (dc) in next st, 3 tr (dc), 2trcl

Figure 35 *Close up of the chevron
pattern contained in the skirt (**figure
28**) and in the dress (**figure 31**)*

75

(2dccl), rep from * 11 [12; 13; 14] times, 1 RtrB (RdcB), 2trcl (2dccl), 3 tr (dc), 2 tr (dc) in last st, 3 ch, turn.
Rep Row 39, 18 times keeping Rtr (Rdc) on rs of work.
Row 58 (inc row) 1 tr (dc) in same place, 5 tr (dc), *1 RtrF (RdcF), 5 tr (dc), 3 tr (dc) in next st, 5 tr (dc), rep from * 11 [12; 13; 14] times, 1 RtrF (RdcF), 5 tr (dc), 2 tr (dc) in last st, 3 ch, turn.
Row 59 1 tr (dc) in same place, 4 tr (dc), 2trcl (2dccl), *1 RtrB (RdcB), 2trcl (2dccl), 4 tr (dc), 3 tr (dc) in next st, 4 tr (dc), 2trcl (2dccl), rep from * 11 [12; 13; 14] times, 1 RtrB (RdcB), 2trcl (2dccl), 4 tr (dc), 2 tr (dc) in last st, 3 ch, turn.
Rep Row 59 to required length, keeping the Rtr (Rdc) on rs of work.
Fasten off.

To make up

Join the 2 pieces together on the ws of one side of the skirt only. Turn the dc (sc) waistband down and attach to form a casing for the elastic. Insert elastic and fasten at side. Join other side seam to within 15cm (6 in) of the top. Insert zip by hand using matching sewing cotton, by first back stitching, then hemming the edges down close (but not too close) to the teeth of the zip.

SUMMER TOP (*figure 36*)

This is definitely *not* a pattern for beginners. One of the pattern processes is to insert the hook into the base of the stitch and figure 37 indicates what is meant and shows where the hook should be placed. Another point to keep in mind with this design is that it looks best when it is slightly stretched over the figure. It is still an effective stitch pattern when hanging loosely but there is more clarity of stitch design when it is very slightly and gently stretched.

Materials
7 balls Robin Reward 3-ply
4.00mm (F) hook

Measurement
To fit bust size 87-92cm (34-36in)

Tension (gauge)
2 patts, measured across widest part of leaf, to 6.5cm (3½in)

Back
Make 104 ch.
Row 1 1 tr (dc) 1 ch 1 tr (dc) in 4th ch from hook, miss 4 ch, *1 dc (sc) in next ch, miss 4 ch, (1 tr [dc] 1 ch) 3 times, 1 tr (dc) in next ch, rep from * to last 5 ch, miss 4 ch, 4 tr (dc) in last ch, 1 ch, turn.
Row 2 1 quad tr (tr tr) in ch, 1 dtr (tr) in base of tr tr (dtr), 1 tr (dc) in base of dtr (tr), 2 ch, 1 htr (hdc) in base of tr (dc), using the same place as the sts up the leaf work 1 tr (dc), 1 dtr (tr), 1 tr tr (dtr) to take you to base of leaf, 1 dc (sc) in centre 1-ch sp of gr of row below. Rep from * to end, 4 ch, turn.
Row 3 Leaving last lp on hook make 1 RdtrF (RtrF) round dtr (tr), 1 RdtrF (RtrF) round htr (hdc), yoh, draw through 3 lps, 3 ch, *1 dc (sc) in 2 ch sp, 3 ch, leaving last lps of each st on hook make 1 RdtrF (RtrF) round tr (dc), 1 RdtrF (RtrF) round tr tr (dtr), 1 RrtrF (RdtrF) round dc (sc), 1 RdtrF (RtrF) round dtr (tr), 1 RdtrF

Figure 36 *This top has a sweet and innocent look to it but is in fact the most difficult stitch pattern in this book*

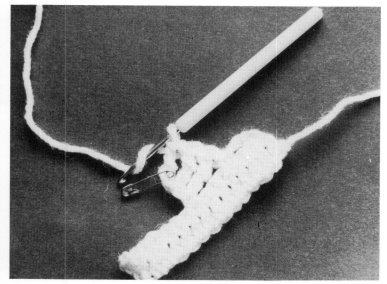

Figure 37 The circle at the base of the drawing pin shows the place to insert the hook to make '1 tr (dc) in base of dtr (tr)'

(RtrF) round htr (hdc), yoh and draw through all 6 lps, 3 ch, rep from * to last leaf top, 1 dc (sc) in 2 ch sp, 3 ch, leaving last lps of each st on hook make 1 RdtrF (RtrF) round tr (dc), 1 RdtrF (RtrF) round tr tr (dtr), 1 tr tr (dtr) in last st, yoh, and draw through all lps.

Row 4 1 tr (dc) 1 ch 1 tr (dc) in same place as turning ch, 1 dc (sc) in dc (sc), *1 tr (dc) 1 ch 1 tr (dc) 1 ch 1 tr (dc) 1 ch 1 tr (dc) in 2-ch sp, 1 dc (sc) in dc (sc), rep from * to top of last leaf, 1 tr (dc) 1 ch 1 tr (dc) 1 ch 1 tr (dc) in last st.

Row 5 As row 2.

Row 6 As row 3 but work raised sts round back.

Rep until patt measures 52cm (20in), finishing with either row 3 or 6. Break off yarn.

Front

Work as for Back until work measures 36cm (14¼in) finishing with either row 3 or 6.

Divide for neck

Next row Work to top of 5th leaf, turn.

Work 2 more rows in patt.

Next row Work 4 complete leaves, turn.

Next row Ss (sl st) to top of leaf, patt to end, turn.

Next row Work in patt.

Next row Ss (sl st) to top of scallop. Work 3 complete leaves.

Work straight until work measures 52cm (20in). Fasten off yarn.

Complete other side to match. Join 2 pieces tog.

SECTION D

VARIATIONS FOR THE PULLOVER

a Work the front in two pieces and add front button bands for a sleeveless cardigan, using 21 ch.

b Add sleeves either by using a dressmaker's sleeve pattern piece for fitted sleeves (p. 61), or by keeping the sides straight to give a dropped sleeve.

Figure 38   *Chevron variation e on
p. 74*

c   Use two balls of DK (worsted) together for the part worked in
chenille.

VARIATIONS FOR THE SKIRT

a   Omit the dc (sc) waistband and commence with the tr (dc) row.
Then attach a strip of belt stiffener or petersham in place of the
elastic.

b   Work the raised trebles as crab st on top of the skirt after it has
been completed.

c   This pattern is ideal for using colour in subtle shadings. Start with
the palest shade at the waist and go darker as the skirt progresses in
length, or, for a more striking effect, use up all your oddments of
4-ply. Remember to work both sides together, however, so that the
colours match at the side seams.

d   Substitute this particular way of working chevrons with one of
the suggestions given in Section B.

e   Make another two pieces for a top. It will be necessary to increase
more quickly for the top than the skirt and obviously these two
pieces will need to be shorter (*figure 38*). These, too, can be shaded
as for the skirt, light at waist and dark at neck.

VARIATIONS FOR THE LEAFY SUMMER TOP

a   Add borders at sleeve and neck edges.

b Work the pattern for the back twice and omit the pattern for the front to give a square neck.

c Thread a cord through the tips of the leaves at waist level for a drawstring and tie.

d Add sleeves, but as the pattern is not one of the easiest to follow and adjust, a simple T-shape is suggested as was designed for the very first top (see p. 19).

e The length from the foundation chain to dividing for the armhole can be extended to give a tunic top or bikini cover-up. If the wearer's hip measurement is larger than her bust it will be necessary to leave the side seams unconnected from a point just below the waist.

TAILORED DESIGN

Garments designed in very soft yarns such as silks, mohairs, llama, and single ply cobweb yarns, which can use a large size hook, do not usually require extra shaping to fit the figure, as it will automatically mould to the body and find its own level of curvature. Firmer yarns, using an average or smaller size hook and a simple close-textured stitch pattern, often benefit from the inclusion of extra fitting points. If the crochet fabric being produced strongly resembles the texture of a piece of woven cloth, it could be advantageous to include extra shaping, but it should be stressed that generally crochet fabrics are not firm enough to need this extra fitting detail. Special shaping may also be an advantage when catering for disproportionate figures. These irregularities can often be accommodated by a change in hook size (see p. 56), but the methods given below are alternatives to changing hook size. They create shape by using the stitches' own heights and/or incorporating increases and decreases.

Shoulders

Sloping shoulders, except in a raglan or yoke style, can be shaped by working the final row as a wedge shape (assuming the crochet is progressing from the waist upwards). The wedge is made of a quarter of the row nearest arm in slip stitch: a quarter of the row in double crochet (single crochet): a quarter of the row in half treble (half double crochet): a quarter of the row nearest neck in treble (double crochet). If shoulders are very sloping or if the work is fine, a matching wedge shaped row can be added to the back.

Armhole bands

As work progresses outwards from the armhole, regular decreasing at the shoulder point gives the band a closer fit to the arm.

Back neck

Wherever there is a rounding of the shoulder blades, decreases can be worked at the two points either side of the back neck, thus curving the crochet into the neck.

Neck bands

Unless a person has a very straight back and erect carriage it is usually necessary to decrease regularly at the two points on the shoulder line at back neck, (*diagram 20*). Also in a fitted round neckline, decrease regularly at the two points either side of the front neck.

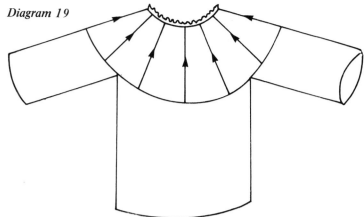

Diagram 19

Sleeves

If extra width has been given to the top part of a sleeve because of a heavy upper arm, it is sometimes difficult to get the sleeve to fit into the shaped armhole. An extra, regular decrease in the centre of the sleeve to act as a dressmaker's dart will help, as will a gathering thread used in the same way that dressmakers use a gathering thread on a sleeve head, to ease the sleeve into the armhole.

Elbows

Darts can be placed at the elbows but this is unnecessary unless the fabric is particularly stiff and unbending (the kind of crochet that is definitely *not* recommended within these pages).

Armholes

As with the elbow there should be no need for armhole darts if a pleasing crochet fabric is being made, unless perhaps the back of the body has as much, if not more, curvature than the front.

Armhole bands

To avoid armhole bands poking at the back and front underarms, decrease regularly at both these places (*diagram 20*).

Bust

Darts coming from the side seam to the bust point can be incorporated using the idea of a wedge shape as on the shoulders. Ideally the bust dart should be formed over three to six rows sloping down towards the side seam.

Midriff

Bust darts can be incorporated by increasing as work progresses upwards from the waist. It is always advisable to use a piece of coloured thread or a safety pin to mark where the increases are to be worked, as the effect being aimed at is a point, (see 63). The very experienced crocheter can aim to make these darts slope slightly towards the side seams as work proceeds in an upward direction.

Back

Back darts increasing from waist upwards to neck and from waist downwards to hips, can be included in a fitted style, and for a hollow back.

Diagram 20

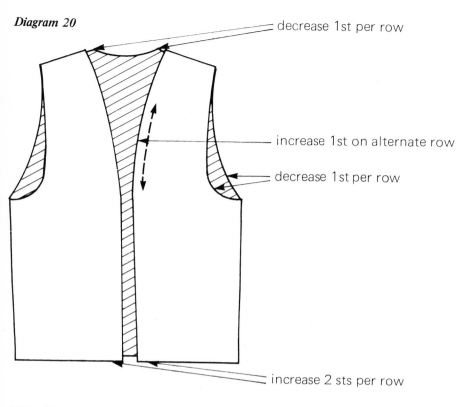

decrease 1st per row

increase 1st on alternate row

decrease 1st per row

increase 2 sts per row

Waist-hip increases

It is worth pointing out again that if only a few points of increase are used for widening the waist measure to the hip measure, there is a tendency for the darts to be noticeable and the fabric to stand stiffly away from the body. To avoid this either stagger the points of increase as when making a circle, or use a larger number of places for the increases.

Try to avoid darts stopping in awkward places on the stomach or bottom as this can accentuate, rather than hide the shape of the figure.

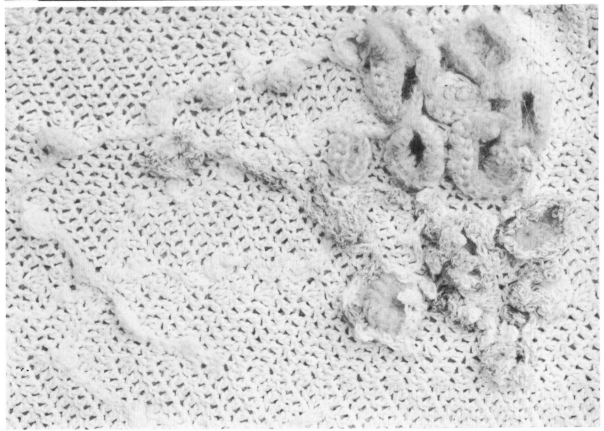

Conclusion

It is not possible to cover all aspects of crochet in these pages, but there is one further technique that I should like to include here which opens the doors to a whole world of creative possibilities, and that is surface crochet.

Surface crochet is work that is put on a foundation, not necessarily a crocheted fabric, after it has been made. There are two methods of doing this.

a With the yarn held below the surface of the fabric. This is a particularly useful method for incorporating letters, names, exact shapes, etc. as it produces an accurate outline of the shape by lying flat along the surface of the fabric when a smooth yarn is used. A textured yarn such as a random dyed bouclé gives a much softer effect (*colour plate 6*).

With the yarn below the fabric only a series of chains can be produced. It is in fact a coarser version of the form of embroidery known as tambour. To work, insert the hook through the right side of the fabric, collecting the yarn from below with the hook head (*figure 39*) and pull through to the right side which is on top, *insert the hook again in a different place and collect the yarn once more in the hook head, pull this yarn through to the right side of the fabric and through the loop on the hook. Repeat from *.

b With the yarn joined to the top of the fabric. Using this method, crunchy textures of all shapes and sizes can be made, creating a truly three-dimensional effect (*figure 40*).

Pinch the fabric together and poke the hook into an available place (*figure 41*). Work the correct number of chain to lift the hook followed by a number of stitches which can be worked on one spot. Any type of stitch can be used and in any combination. The idea is to get a chunky, textured effect, and only experimentation will supply the answers.

Try experimenting with free design, using regular appliquéd motifs as shown in the peacock cloak, (*colour plate 2*), irregular motifs symmetrically placed as on the coat shown in colour plate 7, unusual shaped motifs such as the seascape scene on the waistcoat in figure 42, or following a sketch of simplified lines like the 'heather hills' design (*colour plate 5*).

These are just a few ideas to set your imagination working. The aim of this book has not been to provide an exhaustive list of crochet techniques, but to give you a good grasp of the basic principles and to show you how to set about transforming your ideas into workable patterns. The rest is up to you.

Figure 39 opposite above: Collecting the yarn when working the tambour method of surface crochet

Figure 40 opposite below: Crunchy texture added to a crochet base using the second method of surface crochet

Figure 41 below: Working with the yarn on top of the work to give added height to the furface crochet

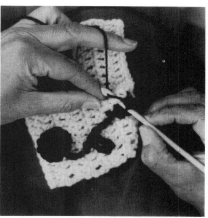

Figure 42 The base and bird motifs are in washable suede – the whole crocheted together mixing yarns as 'the fancy took me'. Stitch heights, increasing and decreasing were all used to keep the work flat

Appendices

I Hook Sizes

INTERNATIONAL STANDARD RANGE (ISR)	UNITED KINGDOM Wool (Old Nos)	Cotton	UNITED STATES Wool	Cotton
10.00mm				
9.00mm	000		15	
	00		13	
8.00mm	0		12	
	1		11	
7.00mm	2		10½ K	
	3		10 J	
6.00mm	4		9 I	
5.50mm	5		8 H	
5.00mm	6		7	
4.50mm	7		6 G	
4.00mm	8		5 F	
3.50mm	9		4 E	
			3 D	
3.00mm	10	3/0	2 C	
	11	2/0		0
2.50mm	12	0	1 B	1
	13	1	0	2
				3
2.00mm	14	1½		4
		2		5
1.75mm		2½		6
		3		
1.50mm		3½		7
		4		8
1.25mm		4½		9
		5		10
1.00mm		5½		11
		6		12
0.75mm		6½		13
0.60mm		7		14
		7½		
		8		

I   International Crochet Symbols

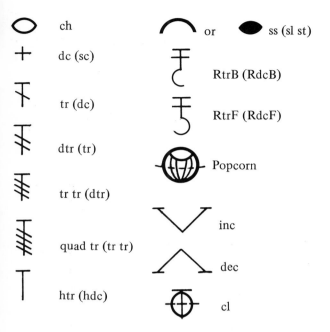

◯ ch	⌢ or ⬤ ss (sl st)
✛ dc (sc)	RtrB (RdcB)
⊤ tr (dc)	RtrF (RdcF)
⧧ dtr (tr)	Popcorn
⧮ tr tr (dtr)	∨ inc
⧲ quad tr (tr tr)	∧ dec
⊤ htr (hdc)	⊕ cl

II   Reading a Commercial Pattern

A commercial pattern often presents a would-be crocheter with problems of interpretation, if for no other reason than because a sequence of movements of the hook taking seconds to execute may take half a page to write. This often results in instructions which have either been so simplified for clarity that the resulting pattern is remarkably uninspired, or so condensed to save space as to be almost incomprehensible.

Another difficulty arises from the diverse forms of expression adopted by crochet designers and although efforts are being made to standarize terms and abbreviations, the situation is further complicated by the relatively high proportion of overseas patterns on the market where the terminology is yet again different.

MATERIALS

The thickness of yarns range from 1-ply cobwebs to the bulky chunky knits. Technically, 'ply' is the number of strands incorporated into a twisted yarn, therefore 2-ply has two strands twisted together to make a single continuous thread, 3-ply has three strands, 4-ply four strands and so on. Chunky yarns, however, have two or three strands twisted, but as each strand is either loosely twisted or just simply thicker it is not referred to as a 2- or 3-ply yarn and cannot be substituted for the yarn in a 2-ply pattern as it is some eight times thicker than the yarn known as 2-ply.

MEASUREMENTS

The standard measurement now being used in the United Kingdom is the metric system (SI units). If only metric sizes are given and you are in doubt as to what the sizes are, use a tape measure which indicates both inches and centimetres, and let the tape measure do the conversion for you.

All sizes will have a movement allowance included, therefore the finished garment should be very slightly in excess of the actual size required. The amount of allowance depends on the type of garment being crocheted. For example, a fitted cotton jacket with sleeves set in requires more movement allowance than a sleeveless waistcoat; conversely, a tabard will require less movement allowance as this garment is often only permanently attached at the shoulders. Any movement allowance included is not as great as that in dressmaking, as woven fabrics do not normally mould themselves around the human figure as easily as crochet.

If a pattern gives instructions for a number of sizes, e.g. bust 76-107cm (30-42in), it helps to underline the size being worked *throughout the pattern* before commencing to crochet.

TENSION (GAUGE)

All patterns include a tension (gauge) check which has been tested by home crocheters and found to be as accurate as possible. It is perhaps the most important single piece of information to be found on the pattern if the article is to finish the size and shape stated, and yet it is frequently ignored.

To check the tension (gauge) of a piece of crochet see p. 15.

THE CHAIN

The chain (see p. 16) initially produced will be longer than the number of stitches required for the base or foundation row. The precise number of extra stitches will be determined by (a) the size of the stitch being used; (b) whether there is to be a chain space to start with; (c) whether there is decreasing or increasing.

As the hook sits on top of the stitch in crochet and as each type of stitch used in crochet is of a different height, it is necessary, at the beginning of a row, to lift the hook to the correct position for working the row by doing a number of turning chains. Unless your tension (gauge) dictates otherwise, the necessary number of chains required to life the hook for a particular stitch is:

Stitch	Number of Turning Chain
ss (sl st)	0
dc (sc)	1
htr (hdc)	2
tr (dc)	3
dtr (tr)	4
tr tr (dtr)	5
quad tr (tr tr)	6

The turning chains will have been added already in a commercially printed pattern, but the pattern may say '*Next row* 1 tr in each st' and omits to inform you that you require a '3 ch turn' prior to working the '1 tr in each st'.

The following are some basic rules applicable to most commercially printed patterns.

a Read *everything* between the commas, e.g. 1 tr (dc) 1 ch 1 tr (dc) into next 2 ch sp, means 'miss all the stitches until the next 2 chain space is reached and then into the hole by the chain of the previous row, work 2 trebles (double crochet) separated by a chain'. In crochet some instructions are very lengthy but an instruction is not completed until the comma is reached.

b Unless specifically told otherwise, a stitch is worked into the next stitch by picking up the top two threads forming a chain along the top of the work, not by placing the hook between the stems of the stitches.

c Instructions written after or between asterisks are repeated a stated number of times. This information is usually clear because the instruction will state 'repeat from * x times'. Thus the instructions are carried out the given number of times plus one, the original, in all.

d Instructions given in brackets, however, may not be quite so clear. Usually the brackets contain the method of producing a particular stitch and a process is bracketed with a number written after it. This means you work the instruction the exact number of times given after the bracket. Occasionally the instruction will say after the bracket 'so many times more' and in this instance work the bracket for the number of times given plus one, (being the original).
e As the turning chain counts as the first stitch in order to keep the edges of the work straight, miss the hole directly at the base of the turning chain and work into the next stitch. At the end of the row it will be necessary to put a stitch in the top of the last of the turning chain of the previous row.

MARKING THE WORK

Often a pattern will say 'right side' (rs) when working a particular row. This is for identification purposes when one later comes to the shaping. As there is rarely a right and wrong side with crochet, it is advisable to put a piece of contrasting yarn through the work, tie the ends with the tails showing at the side the pattern calls 'right side'. This saves a lot of time later when trying to decide which *is* the right side.

Marking work by using a contrasting piece of yarn is a convenient method of marking on other occasions in crochet, e.g.
a at a raglan sleeve edge where the decrease occurs a few stitches in from the edge of the work and where the commencement of the decreasing cannot readily be discerned with a quick glance.
b when increasing or decreasing in a plain fabric for darts, etc. where it is difficult to locate the precise point at which the increase/decrease has to occur.
c when measuring for buttons/buttonholes.
d at the beginning of a round when working motifs.
Marking work with a contrasting yarn is a more advisable method than using a straight pin or even a safety-pin, as these tend to get caught or lost in the fabric.

MEASURING

When measuring the work, place it on a smooth surface so that there will be no temptation to let the crochet cling and stretch and then end up shorter than you intended! Cloth and plastic tape measures become inaccurate with wear and tear so either keep renewing your measure at regular intervals or invest in a retractable metal one. If a large article such as a skirt, coat or dress is being made, it is advisable to hang it whilst work is in progress by evenly pinning it to a padded hanger and covering it with a polythene bag or cotton sheet between the periods of work. This allows the weight of the yarn to pull at it and cause a natural drop to occur, thus saving embarrassment for the wearer. It has been known that what started as a car coat at the beginning of an afternoon's outing ended up as a calf-length coat by the time wearer arrived home!

ARMHOLE SHAPINGS

Armhole shapings when worked exactly as instructed in the pattern, often cause puzzlement, disappointment or concern to a relatively new crocheter. I cannot excuse or condone some of the poor shapings given in a large number of commercial patterns which frequently give an unsatisfactory edge to an armhole. All too often one or both of the decreasing edges result in steps which create unnecessary bulk when attaching the edging or any other part of the garment. This kind of shaping should be avoided, as should one that leaves holes at the edge, as these pull when the edging etc. is attached. Should you find the instructions given in the pattern you are following inadequate, try the method given here (p. 48).

ARMHOLE/NECK/FRONT BANDS

I never cease to be surprised by the number of patterns that say 'Work 6 rows dc (sc) to form a border'. That simple sentence causes untold worry for the beginner. The new crocheters blame themselves for either inaccurate tension (gauge) or below average intelligence because they cannot follow successfully what appears to be the simplest of all instructions.

Six rows of double crochet (single crochet) round an armhole edge without any adjustment can only result in an ill-fitting frilled band that displeases the discerning worker. The way to achieve a good fit is not difficult. In a square armhole decrease one stitch at the shoulder seam point and two stitches at the right-angled corners both at front and back *on every row*. This will ensure the band lies close to the arm.
NB: If the work does frill even after decreasing on every row, there were too many stitches put into the armhole edge on the very first row.

There is no rule of thumb as to how many stitches to work up the side edge of a piece of crochet, as this will depend on many things such as the stitch pattern, the steepness of the slope of decrease, or whether the hook size is the same as that worked for the body of the garment. However, the following is an approximate guide when using the same yarn and the same hook:

In a piece of dc (sc) work 1 dc (sc) into every other row.
In a piece of htr (hdc) work 1 dc (sc) into every row.
In a piece of tr (dc) work 3 dc (sc) into every 2 rows.
In a piece of dtr (tr) work 2 dc (sc) into every row.

To save ugly joins and to give the garment a firm, hard-wearing edge the designer will tell you to work the front, neck and hem border all in one — the instruction to you is still 'work 6 rows dc (sc) to form a border', minus any extra instruction for the inexperienced worker that as the border is having to travel round a right angle at the base of the fronts, it will be necessary to put extra stitches in at the point to enable the border to lie flat. An all-in-one front border requires you to decrease at the inside curves of the neck and increase on the outside curves of the front opening. When there is a right-angled corner such as that at the base where the front meets the hem, place three stitches at the point, on every row. This gives you one stitch for the front border, one stitch for the corner and one stitch for the hem side when you come to work the next row.

FASTENINGS

Buttonholes

A buttonhole is extremely simple in crochet. First decide (perhaps when working your tension [gauge] square) how large your hole has to be for the chosen button, i.e., whether you need one, two, three or four chain. Mark the position of the buttonhole with contrasting marker thread (on the main body of the work if the buttonholes are not worked directly into the front band) and when you reach this point work your row as normal, but omit the central stitches of the band and work chains instead to compensate. That is: if you miss 2 stitches — work 2 chains; if you miss 3 stitches — work 3 chains; and so on. On the return row use the chains as though they were stitches and proceed with the band to the next buttonhole marker.

One point to remember is that buttonholes do work loose in time, so make the hole on the small side. If the yarn being used is soft and easily stretched, or if the fabric stitch being used on the band gives a stretch finish because the hook is large and the stitches loose, it is a good idea to add a firming chain on the inside of the band. This can be done by embroidering a chain on the outside edge of the buttonhole band (but on the inside of the work) from hem to neck.

FASTENERS

Buttons and zips are both suitable for fastening crochet fabric, and old buttons can be covered in crochet with the yarn you have used for the rest of the article. Other types of fasteners such as press-studs, hook and eyes and velcro should be used cautiously, as they tend to catch in the crochet yarn. If a buckle is used, care should be taken that it is not too heavy or it will pull the fabric out of shape.

MAKING UP

In a commercial pattern this section often uses the methods evolved for knitting, with suggestions like back-stitching side seams and sleeve seams or oversewing shoulders and bands, but these methods do not always prove satisfactory and the majority of patterns, realizing this simply say 'join seams'.

Eighty-five per cent of the crochet fabrics produced look neater when seams are crocheted together on the wrong side with a double crochet (single crochet) stitch. This acts like the overlock stitch on a sewing machine, encasing any loose ends as well as neatening any ragged turning chains worked at the edges.

A very lacy pattern looks ugly with a firm, straight joining and therefore a double crochet (single crochet) is not advised in this instance. Instead work an open join using chain and slipstitch.

Ideally work the fronts and backs together thus avoiding side seams.

It is certainly not *wrong* to sew, as opposed to crochet, seams together, but there tends to be more 'give' in a crochet join which flows with the movement of the crocheted fabric when the article is in use.

Washing and Pressing
Follow the instructions for laundering given by manufacturers on their ball bands. Many fabrics can be washed in the washing machine, but almost all should be dried flat. My advice for pressing crochet is to do so only when you have to.

If one presses a textured fabric heavily, the result is an unsatisfactory flattening, producing a different finish from that intended. The following guidelines are to help you decide whether your piece of crochet should be pressed or not.

Press if:
a   using mercerized cotton
b   motifs need to be standardized for joining
c   using pure wool in untextured stitches

Do not press if:
a   the pattern is deliberately textured and will be flattened (mercerized cotton will not noticeably flatten).
b   using courtelle/acrylic which will stretch
c   using courtelle and lurex which tends to melt
d   using mohair as the beauty of mohair is its 'hairiness' which will disappear in pressing
e   using mohair and wool
f   using mohair with wool and nylon

LINING

On the whole, crochet does not require lining, but if you feel that a lining will improve your work, then here are a few guidelines:
a   attach the lining at as few points as possible.
b   make the lining larger than the actual pieces of crochet as there is less give in the lining materials than in the crochet and a movement allowance has to be included.
c   be extremely careful when purchasing the lining that the colour is complementary to the crochet, both in daylight and artificial light. Even in double crochet (single crochet) there are minute holes through which the lining may show, particularly on a dance floor.
d   attach sleeve linings only at the armhole edge unless there is a deep tight cuff.
e   attach a full lining for the trunk of the body only at neck and armholes.
f   attach a skirt lining only at the waistband. If it is attached to the hem of any piece of work (including the sleeve the crochet tends to react in an unpredictable way, twisting in very unexpected directions usually opposite to the way the crochet fabric is moving.

III   Crochet for Left-Handed People

As with right-handed people different methods of learning to crochet suit different people. The following are some ways left-handed people can learn to crochet from right-handed people and text books written for right-handed people.

a   Face the person demonstrating the technique so that you get a mirror-image.

b   Place the right-handed demonstrator or the text-book, sideways on to a mirror and look at the technique through the mirror instead of looking at the person or book.

c   A mature person skilful in quite a number of crafts, usually transposes right-handed actions into left-handed actions automatically. This type of person is best standing behind the right shoulder of the demonstrator.

d   Occasionally a left-handed crocheter can transpose all techniques once the initial chain and first few stitches has been shown by a left-handed person. Although slow and cumbersome if the right-hand person could show the very first steps in a left-handed way, that is the only push that is required before a very competent left-handed crocheter emerges.

e   Finally, to help in a different way, the basic stitches shown in Sections A of Chs II—VII are printed here as though being worked by a left-handed crocheter: **a** holding the yarn, **b** slip knot, **c** chain, **d** slip stitch, **e** double crochet (single crochet), **f** crab stitch, **g** treble (double crochet).

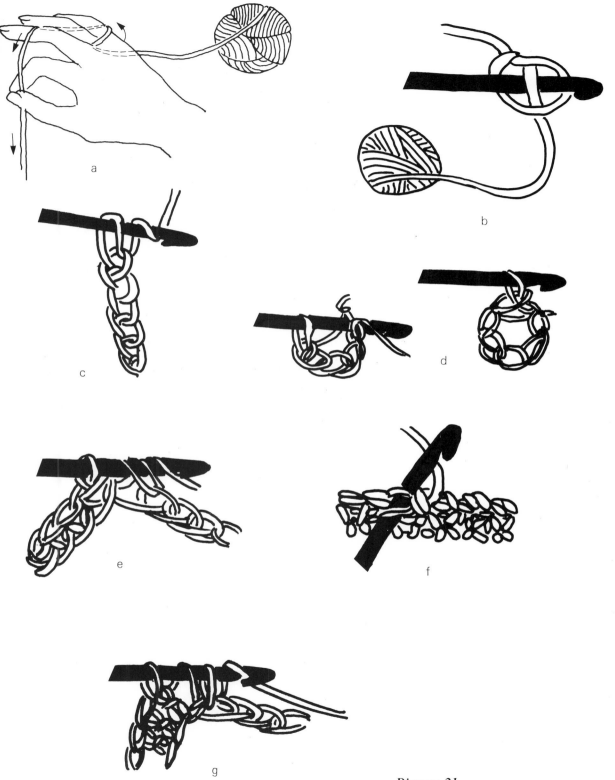

a

b

c

d

e

f

g

Diagram 21

IV Crochet for the Physically Handicapped

Crochet does not use the muscles of the chest or exert pressure on the heart, so people suffering from angina and other chest complaints who have been advised to give up knitting can convert to crochet, which uses the same basic material but a different technique. In fact, crochet is taught in many institutions because of its theraputic value.

It is not within the scope of this present work to explore the many ways in which crochet can be adapted to cope with the skills and requirements of those with physical disabilities, but the story of Mabel sums up the value of crochet to these people. Five years ago, Mabel came to an adult education class with failing eyesight and hands badly knarled and stiff from rheumatism. The smallest hook size that she could hold without it slipping out of her fingers was a 7.00mm (K). Attending classes regularly, Mabel has found her joints gradually loosening up and becoming more supple. She has just crocheted her first mat using a 1.25 (10) hook and Coats No. 10s cotton (*figure 43*). Not only has she mastered the techniques of crochet, but in order to work in 10s cottons, Mabel has to check each round with a magnifying glass, as she crochets by 'feel'.

For further information about crochet for the physically handicapped see *Knitting and Crochet for the Physically Handicapped and Elderly* by Shelagh Hollingworth, Batsford, 1981.

Figure 43 *Mabel's beautiful hands (now!) working fine crochet*

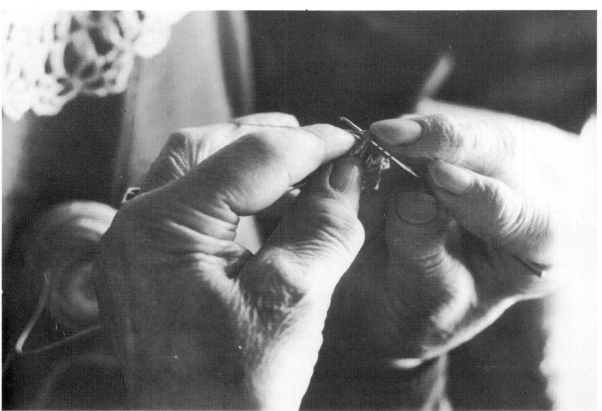

List of Suppliers

UNITED KINGDOM

All yarns are available at good department stores and wool shops throughout the country.
In addition the following sell by mail order:

R.S. Duncan & Co.
Falcon Mills
Bartle Lane
Bradford BD7 4OJ

John Lewis Partnership Ltd
Oxford Street
London W1

William Hall & Co. (Monsall) Ltd
177 Stanley Road
Cheadle Hulme
Cheadle
Cheshire SK8 6RF

The Silver Thimble
33 Gay Street
Bath BA1 2NT

UNITED STATES

Any large nationwide chain store usually stocks yarns and materials but in addition you can obtain supplies by mail order from the following:

American Handicrafts
2617 W. Seventh Street
Fort Worth
Texas 76707

Economy Handicrafts
50-21 69th Street
Woodside
New York 11377

Index